DATE DUE

SE 22 '98		
OC 22 '98		
AP 5 '99		
RENEW		
AP 5 '99		
AP 3 '00		
Apr 26 98		
JE 5 '01		
OC 26 '01		
NO 16 '01		
JE 06 '02		
DE 10 03		
AE 6 03		
AU 13 08		
MY 1 5 '09		

DEMCO 38-296

FEMINISM, PHILOSOPHY, AND THE LAW

EDITED BY LESLIE FRANCIS

THE PENNSYLVANIA STATE UNIVERSITY PRESS
UNIVERSITY PARK, PENNSYLVANIA

Library of Congress Cataloging-in-Publication Data

Date rape : feminism, philosophy, and the law / edited by Leslie
    Francis.

     p.   cm.
    Includes bibliographical references and index.
    ISBN 0-271-01428-8 (cloth)
    ISBN 0-271-01429-6 (paper)
    1. Acquaintance rape—United States.   2. Sex and law—United
States.   3. Law reform—United States.   4. Feminism—United States.
I. Francis, Leslie, 1946–   .
    KF9329.D38   1996
    364.1′532—dc20   95-46944
                                                                      CIP

It is the policy of The Pennsylvania State University Press to use acid-free
paper for the first printing of all clothbound books. Publications on un-
coated stock satisfy the minimum requirements of American National Standard for Information Sciences—Permanence of Paper for Printed Library Materials, ANSI Z39.48—1992.

Contents

Introduction

Leslie Francis

Rape is criminal. Rape is gendered. Rape is sexual. In yet another three-word sentence, rape is controversial. As a crime, rape is viewed more ambiguously than many other offenses. As a social issue, rape reflects deep divisions in our attitudes about sexuality and gender. Sexual violence, inflicted by shadowy strangers leaping out from the dark, is a serious criminal offense—although not judged sufficiently serious to warrant the death penalty.[1] Yet even victims of these "real rapes"[2] may be vilified, more subtly but no less powerfully than the rape victims of the past who were spurned by their husbands.[3] Women who assert that they have

1. See *Coker v. Georgia*, 433 U.S. 584 (1977).
2. The term comes from Susan Estrich, *Real Rape* (Cambridge: Harvard University Press, 1987).
3. Susan Brownmiller, *Against Our Will: Men, Women, and Rape* (New York: Simon & Schuster, 1975).

been victimized by acquaintances—or, worse, by spouses or former lovers—may be met with support, with derision, or with the judgment that they too bear responsibility for what happened. From Mike Tyson to the Portland Trail Blazers to William Kennedy Smith, allegations of acquaintance rape have been high-profile, public events, drawing prurient fascination, condemnation, and even admiration. As this volume goes to press, Mike Tyson has returned victoriously to the ring, apparently unscathed by his conviction and incarceration.

Twenty years ago, Susan Brownmiller's *Against Our Will: Men, Women, and Rape,* brought feminist attention to the history, sociology, and criminal law of rape. Brownmiller argues that rape is a crime of violence, not of passion. In sweeping and powerful descriptions of rape in war, in pogroms, and in slavery, Brownmiller argues that rape is "nothing more or less than a conscious process of intimidation by which *all men* keep *all women* in a state of fear."[4] Her book details the occurrence of rape during the Second World War, the struggle of Bangladesh for independence from Pakistan, and the war in Vietnam. In American history, the rapes of Native American women by white men, and of black women slaves by their white masters, are particular instances of dominance by means of sex. The contemporary rapes of Muslim women in Bosnia, aimed at both humiliation and impregnation, add yet another sad chapter of the sexual oppression of women in war.

The decades since Brownmiller wrote have brought two major waves of rape law reform in the United States.[5] The first wave dealt mainly with legal obstacles to proving that the crime occurred. These obstacles were formidable. In many jurisdictions, the standards of proof for rape were different and higher than for other crimes. Proof of rape, for example, frequently required evidence of the victim's resistance, or corroboration beyond the victim's own testimony. Proof of robbery, by contrast, required no such additional testimony; it was simply left up to the trier of fact to weigh the credibility of the victim's testimony against other evidence in the case. These requirements reflected the problematic judgment that the complainant's credibility in rape cases was inherently

4. Ibid., 15.

5. See Linda A. Fairstein, *Sexual Violence: Our War Against Rape* (New York: William Morrow, 1993).

more suspect than credibility in other cases. Some jurisdictions also required "fresh complaints" of rape—that is, cases reported immediately after the occurrence—on the assumption that outraged victims would be more likely to report attacks immediately (despite their likely fear or shame) and that liars would be more likely to make up their stories at a distance. Many jurisdictions admitted testimony about the victim's prior sexual history as relevant to judging credibility or consent to the sexual act.[6]

In the first wave of reforms, these requirements of proof came under attack. Many jurisdictions abolished the requirements of resistance or corroboration, and these requirements remain in only a distinct minority of states.[7] Another frequent reform was the adoption of what are called "rape shield laws," which limit to varying degrees the admissibility of the victim's prior sexual history in rape trials. The broadest of these shield statutes deny admission of testimony regarding the victim's prior sexual history, except for earlier conduct with the defendant.[8] Other statutes are designed to restrict testimony regarding prior sexual history to various categories of relevance. New York's rape shield law is an example. The law allows the victim to be asked about specific instances of prior sexual conduct with the accused and about whether she has been convicted of prostitution within the past three years. If the prosecution admits evidence of the victim's chastity (for example, to explain her naiveté in describing the events) or of transmittal of sexual disease allegedly because of the rape, the defense may also introduce evidence about prior sexual history in rebuttal. Finally, New York has a general but apparently infrequently used exception for evidence that is admissible in the interests of justice.[9]

This first wave of reform took aim at difficulties in proving the crime rather than at the crime itself. The second wave of rape reform legislation moved beyond issues of proof, to questioning the

6. A good history of the requirements of proof in rape cases is in Estrich, *Real Rape,* 41ff.

7. Kathanne W. Greene, "Rape Reform Legislation in the United States and Canada 1980–1987" (paper presented at the annual meeting of the Western Political Science Association, Salt Lake City, Utah, April 1989).

8. Leigh Bienen, "National Developments in Rape Reform Legislation," *Women's Rights Law Reporter* 6 (1980), 170–213.

9. Fairstein, *Sexual Violence,* 123–24.

very understanding of rape itself. In *Real Rape,* Susan Estrich argued that rapes committed by acquaintances are as real as the rapes inflicted by lurking strangers—even though they are often not recognized as such, either by formal definitions in the criminal law or by juries or judges applying these formal provisions. A number of jurisdictions have amended rape laws to include spousal rape, either in all cases or in situations in which the husband and wife have taken steps toward separation or divorce. Jurisdictions have also adopted statutes defining degrees of sexual assault. Typical statutes graduate the offense by the kind and amount of force used, the age differential between the victim and the offender, the nature of the sexual acts committed, and the relationship between the victim and the offender.[10]

Yet despite these reforms, there remain ambivalence and disagreement about the definition and gradation of criminal sexual assault. One recently published study, based on older data, suggests that gender, race, income level, and residence in areas with high reported crime rates may all influence perceptions of what factors are relevant to deciding whether an aggressive sexual action should be included within the definition of rape. The study presented vignettes to a randomly selected, stratified sample of black and white residents of Los Angeles, California. White females were most likely to regard information about force as relevant to deciding whether a vignette described a rape, and to classify vignettes as rape overall. Black males were least likely to label sexual encounters as rape, and most likely to cite information on resistance by the victim as relevant to their judgments.[11] The study was small, and the data were collected in 1979. The attitudes described surely reflect problematic social variables, not the least of which is that living in a high crime area was negatively associated with judging a vignette to describe rape.[12] The significance of this study for legal reform at the present time is thus problematic. Nonetheless, other studies also report variations in the perception of what is rape, by gender, age, ethnicity, attitudes toward sex, education, and other socioeconomic variables.[13] These data too are

10. Linda Brookover Bourque, *Defining Rape* (Durham, N.C.: Duke University Press, 1989), 111.

11. Ibid., 228–30.

12. Ibid., 216.

13. Ibid., 131–70.

fragmentary, but they are cause for concern about the fairness of radical redefinition of the criminal law of sexual assault to include all unwanted sexual encounters, at least in advance of better knowledge about cultural differences in attitudes toward rape, and possible mechanisms for encouraging attitudinal change. On the other side, legal reform itself is a powerful engine for generating attitudinal change.

Against this background of debate and legal reform, American colleges and secondary schools have witnessed vastly increasing concern about the phenomenon of acquaintance rape. A 1985 study published in *Ms.* magazine argued that one-fourth of college women are victims of rape or attempted rape.[14] This study and several others reporting similarly high assault figures have been questioned because of the scope of their definitions of rape; they tend to include sexual acts which were, on the one hand, unwanted or nonconsensual but, on the other hand, not categorized as rape by the women involved either.[15] Colleges and schools have developed educational and counseling programs for both women and men and have in some cases adopted stringent regulatory policies. Perhaps the strictest policy is Antioch College's student government policy, which requires students to obtain explicit consent for every step of sexual intimacy, including varying degrees of foreplay. A copy of the current version of the policy is included in this volume.[16]

This intense concern about acquaintance rape on campus has brought predictable backlash. Katie Roiphe's *The Morning After*[17] is a scathing critique of at least some feminist approaches to date rape and sexual harassment. Roiphe argues that the furor over date rape perpetuates a stereotype of women as vulnerable, naive, and in need of protection. In the fashion of classic paternalism, it limits the opportunity to experiment or to be spontaneous. Roiphe writes:

> The difficulty with these rules [about rape and sexual harassment] is that, although it may infringe on the right to

14. Mary Koss, "Date Rape: The Story of an Epidemic and Those Who Deny It," *Ms. Magazine,* October 1985.

15. See, e.g., Neil Gilbert, "Realities and Mythologies of Rape," *Society* 29 (1992).

16. See Appendix 1.

17. Katie Roiphe, *The Morning After: Sex, Fear, and Feminism on Campus* (New York: Little, Brown, 1993).

comfort, unwanted sexual attention is part of nature. To find wanted sexual attention, you have to give and receive a certain amount of unwanted sexual attention. Clearly, the truth is that if no one was ever allowed to risk offering unsolicited sexual attention, we would all be solitary creatures.[18]

Lois Pineau's article "Date Rape: A Feminist Analysis," the centerpiece of this volume, is a major contribution to the second wave of reform, the project of rethinking rape. This paper, first published in *Law and Philosophy* in 1989, won the 1992 Berger Memorial Prize of the American Philosophical Association for the best recent paper published in philosophy of law. It was selected for this honor in part because of the innovative philosophical perspective it brings to bear on the project of rethinking the criminalization of sexual assault.

Pineau begins with a definition of date rape as nonconsensual sex that does not involve physical injury or the threat of physical injury. Thus she takes as her subject the kind of sexual encounter for which there is least agreement about the appropriateness of legal prohibition. Pineau's goal is to argue for the criminalization of nonconsensual sex among acquaintances by developing a model of communicative sexuality. She starts by criticizing the first wave of legal reforms for not going far enough to purge the law of deeply gendered injustice toward women. The reforms in the second wave, which define a range of lesser sexual assaults, are also flawed because they still require proof of the offender's *mens rea:* either the belief—or in more enlightened jurisdictions, the reasonable belief—that the victim was not consenting. Their focus is what the man actually thought or what he reasonably could have thought. But in Pineau's view, the spotlight in deciding whether a rape occurred should be directed toward the woman, toward whether or not she actually consented to the sexual encounter. We should work backward from actual consent to an understanding of when it is reasonable for the man to believe that there was consent, and thus to an understanding of criminal sexual assault that does not depend on gendered attitudes about reasonableness.

So Pineau sets out to develop a criterion for consensual sex. Her view is that it is not reasonable for women to agree to coerced or

18. Ibid., 87.

pressured sex (or therefore for men to believe that women have agreed). Her strategy for arguing this is to develop the picture of sexual relationships that plausibly underlies the contrary view, that pressured sex can be consensual. In current gendered attitudes about sex, Pineau writes: "It is extraordinarily difficult for us to distinguish between assault and seduction, submission and enjoyment, or so we imagine."[19] If aggression and submission are part of our view of what is "normal" seduction, then many examples of pressured sex will be viewed as consensual (or at least as situations in which it was reasonable for the man to believe that the woman was consenting). But, Pineau argues, this picture rests on an interlocking set of myths about female provocation and its significance, and about male self-control.

Pineau then seeks to dispel these myths and to replace them with a model of communicative sexuality. In sexual relationships, like in other intimate relationships such as friendship, each person has a duty to respect the other. Respect consists of understanding and trying to further the other's ends. Sexual pleasure—"good sex"—thus requires communication. Each partner should be trying to understand the aims of the other, and to further these ends. Aggressive or coercive sex, or sex that turns aggressive or coercive partway along, lacks this fundamental understanding. It is, therefore, sex to which it would not be reasonable for the woman to consent (since it would not be "good sex") and sex to which it is not reasonable for the man to believe she is consenting.

From this understanding of communicative sexuality, Pineau suggests a new account of the crime of sexual assault. When sexuality is not communicative, it is not reasonable for the man to believe the woman is consenting. If he nevertheless pursues sexual activity, he acts either out of reckless disregard for the woman's desires or out of willful ignorance of what her desires might be— for he cannot know, except through the practice of communicative sexuality, whether his partner has any sexual reason for continuing the encounter. The mental element for the crime of sexual assault is, then, established when it can be shown that the sexuality was not communicative. If in addition there was an act of sexual aggression to which the woman did not consent, the crime of sexual assault has occurred. Sexual assault, in sum, has two elements:

19. See Chapter 1, p. 6.

nonconsensual sexual action without the communication needed to establish that the action was consensual.

This is a radical reconceptualization of sexual assault, as Pineau's commentators point out. Two of the commentators (Angela Harris and Catharine Wells) are lawyers; two (David Adams and Wells) are philosophers, and all three are in some sense feminist theorists. It is fair to say that they agree with Pineau both about the problematic state of much current rape law and about the desirability of communicative sexuality. Where they disagree with Pineau is, first, on the status of communicative sexuality as a model of desirable sex and, second, on the advisability of using communicative sexuality as a basis for legal reform.

Let me take up first the status of communicative sexuality as a model of desirable sex. Both Adams and Wells ask whether communicative sexuality is a unique model of morally acceptable sex. Communicative sexuality as Pineau presents it might be a model of ideal sex, but should it be a model for all sex? Adams's focus is Pineau's contention that communicative sexuality is presumptively reasonable, and hence the kind of sex to which it is reasonable to believe that the woman is consenting; and that noncommunicative, aggressive sexuality is presumptively unreasonable, and hence the kind of sex to which it is not reasonable to believe that there has been consent, absent special evidence to rebut the presumption of nonconsensuality. Adams in effect presents Pineau with a dilemma about reasonableness. For a radical feminist such as Catharine MacKinnon, even communicative sexuality takes place against a background of the disempowerment of women and the use of sexuality as an instrument of oppression. Against this background, even communication about each other's goals is not sufficient to establish the reasonableness of consent to a sexual relationship. For a liberal feminist theorist, on the other hand, the problem with Pineau's position is the implicit paternalism of her claim that it is only reasonable for women to consent to communicative sexuality. If some women enjoy domination, Adams argues, it is questionable whether communicativeness is necessary for reasonableness. So Adams poses a dilemma for Pineau: either there are elements of false consciousness even in communicative sexuality, or it may be reasonable for women to consent to sex that is not very communicative at all.

From a feminist perspective, Wells criticizes Pineau's position as essentialist. Pineau assumes one model of good sex. But Wells suggests we need to ask what women—actual women—want from their sexual experiences. We may find more differences than we expect—from romance novels to the reasonableness admired by Pineau. Like Adams, Wells points out that Pineau is forced to say to readers of the romance[20] that theirs is a false consciousness.

In reply to these concerns about difference, Pineau explains that in her view noncommunicative sex can be consensual from the woman's point of view, if the man has made efforts to ascertain her goals and she has communicated that she desires noncommunicative sex. Suppose, however, that there are women who do not even want the initial discussion about the desirability of communication—just as, perhaps, some people do not want to discuss informed consent to health care. Surely it is regrettable that there are women who prefer the silent world of sex, just as there are patients who prefer the silent world of doctor and patient,[21] but is it utterly irrational?

Judgments about whether Pineau's reply is successful reach deep issues about liberal theory and the nature of the self. Pineau's paradigm is ongoing autonomy: women understanding, communicating, thinking, and rethinking their goals. Anything less is false consciousness. In this, her philosophical roots reach back to Kant. Yet if some kinds of lives are incompatible with this paradigm of the autonomous self, or if the paradigm itself is flawed,[22] Pineau's reply is too easy.

One frequent objection to the paradigm of autonomy is that it abstracts the self from context. There surely are many questions about whether Pineau's discussion is too removed from the multi-

20. See Janice A. Radway, *Reading the Romance: Women, Patriarchy, and Popular Literature* (Chapel Hill: University of North Carolina Press, 1991).

21. The phrase is drawn from Jay Katz's *The Silent World of Doctor and Patient* (New York: The Free Press, 1984), a powerful criticism of physicians' failures to open communication with patients.

22. There is a large debate about Kantian autonomy as the model for the self, and in particular about John Rawls's use of that model in his *Theory of Justice* (Cambridge: Harvard University Press, 1971). For a criticism of the model of the self as freely choosing and rechoosing ends, from a communitarian perspective, see Michael Sandel, *Liberalism and the Limits of Justice* (New York: Cambridge University Press, 1982). For a fine discussion of autonomy with feminist implications, see Thomas Hill, "Servility and Self-Respect," *The Monist* 57 (1973), 87–105.

ple contexts in which sexual relationships occur. Along these lines, Wells also argues, again from a feminist perspective, that Pineau's discussion is utopian, in the classic sense that it fails to pay attention to the real dynamics of power relationships between men and women. In order to understand the consensuality or non-consensuality of sexual relationships, Wells contends, we need deeper consideration of the ranges of choices that really are available to women. Some women, for better or worse, cannot simply rewrite their sexuality on blank slates. Communicative difficulties may be endemic among those who are powerless; indeed, these difficulties may help in explaining desires to avoid communication altogether. If Pineau's model ignores these difficulties, however, it may harm the powerless and make it more difficult for women who lack communicative skills to gain control over their own sexuality. Like other forms of utopianism, Pineau's has reformist aims, but the project of reform may be differently complex in different contexts.

The problems of reform are likewise apparent in Pineau's proposal for legal change. Both Wells and Harris raise serious questions about using Pineau's model of communicative sexuality in defining the criminal law of sexual assault, at least against the background that it is also a call for reform of current social attitudes toward sexuality. Underlying their concerns is the issue of fairness in criminal law. Because the man will be punished, Wells contends, it is his culpability and his mental state that matters. So objective reasonableness should be the standard for judging whether it was reasonable for him to believe that the woman was consenting, and, in addition, whether it was reasonable for him to have done more to find out whether she was consenting. Pineau's proposal, however, ties the reasonableness of the man's belief to the reasonableness of the woman's consent—that is, to whether there was sufficient communication for her apparent acquiescence to have been reasonable consent. Wells is more optimistic than Pineau about the ability of the law to work out a standard of objective reasonableness that is not self-serving—a difference, like several others, that may be related to Wells's legal background.

One of Harris's principal concerns lies in the extent to which Pineau edges away from including a mental element—a *mens rea* requirement—in the crime of rape at all. Pineau is quite attracted to viewing sexual assault as a strict liability offense. On this view, criminal sexual assault has occurred if the man engages in sexual activity with a woman who was in fact not consenting to the activity—whatever his state of mind about her consent. This attraction to strict liability for sexual assault is most apparent in Pineau's reply. Her original article argues for reunderstanding the reasonableness of the man's belief in terms of the reasonableness of the woman's acquiescence, but not abandoning a reasonable belief inquiry altogether. Indeed, Pineau might find it difficult to abandon the reasonable belief inquiry altogether, given what she says about women who apparently want aggressive sex. For her argument, as sketched above, is that aggressive or romanticized sex can fit the communicative model when the man has made efforts to ascertain that this is what the woman wants. Harris's objection to defining sexual assault as a strict liability offense is more general. In the criminal law, there are very few strict liability offenses— principally regulatory offenses that carry fines as punishment and that do not carry suggestions of moral blameworthiness. Sexual assault, by contrast, is punishable by imprisonment, and this would not change under Pineau's proposal. Sexual offenses also are met with opprobrium, and should remain so. Indeed, there is a risk that moving sexual assault toward a strict liability offense would dilute the moral criticism it now receives.

What lies behind the differences between Pineau and her critics? One factor is that Pineau is not a lawyer and that some of her critics are. Lawyers think about the need to formulate general rules that can be put into practice in institutionalized form. They worry about problems of evidence, as Harris's careful discussion reveals. They try to design mechanisms to link criminal punishment to fault. Hence lawyers worry about due process and the rights of the accused, factors that Pineau assigns less weight in the face of the sexual oppression of women. Pineau writes: "It is far more important to remedy this situation [the risks to women from date rape] than it is to avoid convicting some aggressive dolt of a misdemeanor just because he was too clued out to know that he should treat resistance as a form of denial." And Pineau worries a great deal more than lawyers do about the importance of social change. She is criticized for pushing the law in advance of changes in social attitudes about sexual relations. Yet this is exactly where Pineau believes the law should be. For Pineau, even the criminal law has a significant educative function; for her critics, this function must lag behind changes in understanding, at least when criminal punishment is at stake.

Other differences relate to ways of thinking about feminism. All the writers in this volume are in some sense feminists, but they raise quite different feminist themes. On the one hand, some of the discussion draws on a liberal feminist emphasis on women's choices, even for bad sex, and on the social conditions that make choices possible. On the other hand, the discussion also draws on the radical feminist criticism of sexual relations as relations of dominance. Pineau's own view is radical in her aim of rethinking sexuality and sexual relationships. But she is less radical than she could be, since, as her critics point out, she appears ready to accept communication at face value, rather than probing deeper questions about whether the communication itself was obtained on problematic terms.

Still other differences may stem from Pineau's views of autonomy and respect. Pineau relies on an abstract model of autonomy to develop her account of desirable intimate relationships. She sees even sexual pleasure—"good sex"—as arising from the partners' respect for each other's aims. Others of the writers are more contextualist. Wells, for example, is a pragmatist who analyzes sexual relationships in their various social contexts.

Pineau and her critics all agree, however, on the need for further reform of the law of sexual assault. They also agree on the need for major changes in sexual attitudes, changes that may bring with them further possibilities for legal reform. Herein lies the greatest significance of Pineau's work: its radical challenge to acceptance of aggressive sexuality that fails to respect persons.

In the early 1990s, Antioch College, a small residential liberal arts college in Ohio, developed a consent to sexual relations policy that received widespread national attention. The goal of the policy is to ensure that sexual relations among students at the college are informed and consensual. The Antioch policy is so appropriate as an illustration of the consensual sexuality that Pineau defends, that we sought approval from the college to include it in this volume as Appendix 1. Because the policy was a lightning rod for controversy, an article defending the policy and addressed to Antioch alumni, students, and parents of students, by Antioch's president at the time, Alan E. Guskin, is included as Appendix 2. Appendix 3 is an analysis of the policy in terms of Pineau's approach and liberal theory by a philosopher, Matthew R. Silliman.

1

Date Rape:
A Feminist Analysis

Lois Pineau

The feminist recognition that dominant ideologies reinforce conceptual frameworks that serve patriarchal interests lies behind what must now be seen as a revolution in political analysis, one which for the first time approaches the problems that women face from a woman's point of view. One of those problems is the ongoing difficulty of dealing with a society that practices and condones violence against women. This is particularly the case with date rape.

Date rape is nonaggravated sexual assault, nonconsensual sex that does not involve physical injury or the explicit threat of physi-

This chapter, which was awarded the Fred Berger Memorial Prize of the American Philosophical Association in 1992 as the best article in the philosophy of law, first appeared in *Law and Philosophy* 8 (1989), 217–43, © 1989 Kluwer Academic Publishers. Reprinted here by permission of Kluwer Academic Publishers.

cal injury. But because it does not involve physical injury, and because physical injury is often the only criterion that is accepted as evidence that the *actus reas* is nonconsensual, what is really sexual assault is often mistaken for seduction. The replacement of the old rape laws with the new laws on sexual assault have done nothing to resolve this problem.

Rape, defined as nonconsensual sex, usually involving penetration by a man of a woman who is not his wife, has been replaced in some criminal codes with the charge of sexual assault.[1] This has the advantage of extending both the range of possible victims of sexual assault and the manner in which people can be assaulted, and replacing a crime which is exclusive of consent with one for which consent is a defense.[2] But while the consent of a woman is now consistent with the conviction of her assailant in cases of aggravated assault, nonaggravated sexual assault is still distinguished from normal sex solely by the fact that it is not consented to. Thus the question of whether someone has consented to a sexual encounter is still important, and the criterion for consent continues to be the central concern of discourse on sexual assault.[3]

However, if a man is to be convicted, it does not suffice to establish that the *actus reas* was nonconsensual. In order to be guilty of sexual assault, a man must have the requisite *mens rea,* i.e., he must have believed either that his victim did not consent or that she was probably not consenting.[4] In many common law jurisdictions, a man who sincerely believes that a woman consented to a sexual encounter is deemed to lack the required *mens rea,* even though the woman did not consent and even though his belief is

1. G. Geis and R. Geis, "Rape Reform: An Appreciative-Critical Review," *Bulletin of the American Academy of Psychiatry and the Law* 6:301–12. Also see Michael Davis, "Setting Penalties: What Does Rape Deserve?" *Law and Philosophy* 3:61–110.

2. Under common law a person cannot consent to aggravated assault. Also, consent may be irrelevant if the victim was unfit to consent. See Davis, "Setting Penalties," 104–5.

3. Discussion Paper No. 2, *Rape and Allied Offenses: Substantive Aspects,* Law Reform Commission of Victoria, August 1986.

4. In a recent Australian case a man was convicted of being an accomplice to a rape because he was reckless in determining whether the woman raped by his friend was consenting. The judge ruled that his "reckless indifference" sufficed to establish *mens rea.* This ruling was possible, however, only because unreasonable belief is not a rape defense in Australia. See *Australian Law Review* 71:120.

not reasonable.[5] Recently, strong dissenting voices have been raised against the sincerity condition, and the argument made that *mens rea* be defeated only if the defendant has a reasonable belief that the plaintiff consented.[6] The introduction of legislation which excludes "honest belief" (unreasonable sincere belief) as a defense will certainly help to provide women with greater protection against violence. But while this will be an important step forward, the question of what constitutes a reasonable belief, the problem of evidence when rapists lie, and the problem of the entrenched attitudes of the predominantly male police, judges, lawyers, and jurists who handle sexual assault cases remains.

The criteria for *mens rea,* for the reasonableness of belief, and for consent are closely related. For although a man's sincere belief in the consent of his victim may be sufficient to defeat *mens rea,* the court is less likely to believe his belief is sincere if his belief is unreasonable. If his belief is reasonable, they are more likely to believe in the sincerity of his belief. But evidence of the reasonableness of his belief is also evidence that consent really did take place. For the very things that make it reasonable for *him* to believe that the defendant consented are often the very things that incline the court to believe that she consented. What is often missing is the voice of the woman herself, an account of what it would be reasonable for *her* to agree to—that is to say, an account of what is reasonable from *her* standpoint.

Thus, what is presented as reasonable has repercussions for four separate but related concerns: (1) the question of whether a man's belief in a woman's consent was reasonable; (2) the problem of whether it is reasonable to attribute *mens rea* to him; (3) the question of what could count as reasonable from the woman's point of view; and (4) the question of what is reasonable from the court's point of view. These repercussions are of the utmost practical concern. In a culture which contains an incidence of sexual assault verging on epidemic, a criterion of reasonableness which regards

5. This is true, at present, in jurisdictions which follow the precedent set by *Morgan v. Morgan.* In this case, four men were acquitted of rape because they sincerely thought that their victim had consented, despite their admitting that she had protested vigorously. See Mark Thornton's "Rape and *Mens Rea," Canadian Journal of Philosophy,* supp. vol. 8:119–46.

6. Ibid.

mere submission as consent fails to offer persons vulnerable to those assaults adequate protection.

The following statements by self-confessed date rapists reveal how our lack of a solution for dealing with date rape protects rapists by failing to provide their victims with legal recourse:

> All of my rapes have been involved in a dating situation where I've been out with a woman I know. . . . I wouldn't take no for an answer. I think it had something to do with my acceptance of rejection. I had low self-esteem and not much self-confidence and when I was rejected for something which I considered to be rightly mine, I became angry and I went ahead anyway. And this was the same in any situation, whether it was rape or it was something else.[7]

> When I did date, when I was younger, I would pick up a girl and if she didn't come across I would threaten her or slap her face then tell her she was going to fuck—that was it. But that's because I didn't want to waste time with any come-ons. It took too much time. I wasn't interested because I didn't like them as people anyway, and I just went with them just to get laid. Just to say that I laid them.[8]

There is, at this time, nothing to protect women from this kind of unscrupulous victimization. A woman on a casual date with a virtual stranger has almost no chance of bringing a complaint of sexual assault before the courts. One reason for this is the prevailing criterion for consent. According to this criterion, consent is implied unless some emphatic episodic sign of resistance occurred and its occurrence can be established. But if no episodic act occurred, or if it did occur and the defendant claims that it didn't, or if the defendant threatened the plaintiff but won't admit it in court, it is almost impossible to find any evidence that would support the plaintiff's word against the defendant. This difficulty is exacerbated by suspicion on the part of the courts, police, and legal educators that even where an act of resistance occurs this act should

---

7. *Why Men Rape,* ed. Sylvia Levine and Joseph Koenig (Toronto: Macmillan, 1980), 83.
8. Ibid., 77.

not be interpreted as a withholding of consent, and this suspicion is especially upheld where the accused is a man who is known to the female plaintiff.

In Glanville Williams's classic textbook on criminal law we are warned that where a man is unknown to a woman she does not consent if she expresses her rejection in the form of an episodic and vigorous act at the "vital moment." But if the man is known to the woman she must, according to Williams, make use of "all means available to her to repel the man."[9] Williams warns that women often welcome a "mastery advance" and present a token resistance. He quotes Byron's couplet:

> A little still she strove, and much repented
> And whispering "I will ne'er consent"—consented

by way of alerting law students to the difficulty of distinguishing real protest from pretense.[10] Thus, while in principle a firm unambiguous stand or a healthy show of temper ought to be sufficient, if established, to show nonconsent, in practice the forceful overriding of such a stance is apt to be taken as an indication that the resistance was not seriously intended and that the seduction had succeeded. The consequence of this is that it is almost impossible to establish the defendant's guilt beyond a reasonable doubt.

Thus, on the one hand, we have a situation in which women are vulnerable to the most exploitive tactics at the hands of men who are known to them. On the other hand, almost nothing will count as evidence of their being assaulted, including their having taken an emphatic stance in withholding their consent. The new laws have done almost nothing to change this situation. Yet some solution must be sought. Moreover, the road to that solution presents itself clearly enough as a need for a reformulation of the criterion of consent. It is patent that a criterion that collapses whenever the crime itself succeeds will not suffice.

The purpose of this paper is to develop such a criterion, and I propose to do so by grounding this criterion in a conception of the "reasonable." Part of the strength of the present criterion for consent lies in the belief that it is reasonable for women to agree to

9. Williams, *Textbook of Criminal Law* (1983), 238.
10. Ibid.

the kind of sex involved in "date rape," or that it is reasonable for men to think that they have agreed. My argument is that it is not reasonable for women to consent to that kind of sex and that there are, furthermore, no grounds for thinking that it is reasonable. Since what we want to know is when a woman has consented, and since standards for consent are based on the presumed choices of reasonable agents, it is what is reasonable from a woman's point of view that must provide the principal delineation of a criterion of consent that is capable of representing a woman's willing behavior. Developing this line of reasoning further, I will argue that the kind of sex to which it would be reasonable for women to consent suggests a criterion of consent that would bring the kind of sex involved in date rape well within the realm of sexual assault.

The Problem of the Criterion

The reasoning that underlies the present criterion of consent is entangled in a number of mutually supportive mythologies which see sexual assault as masterful seduction, and silent submission as sexual enjoyment. Because the prevailing ideology has so much informed our conceptualization of sexual interaction, it is extraordinarily difficult for us to distinguish between assault and seduction, submission and enjoyment, or so we imagine. At the same time, this failure to distinguish has given rise to a network of rationalizations that support the conflation of assault with seduction, submission with enjoyment. I therefore want to begin my argument by providing an example which shows both why it is so difficult to make this distinction and that it exists. Later, I will identify and attempt to unravel the lines of reasoning that reinforce this difficulty.

> The woman I have in mind agrees to see someone because she feels an initial attraction to him and believes that he feels that same way about her. She goes out with him in the hope that there will be mutual enjoyment and in the course of the day or evening an increase of mutual interest. Unfortunately, these hopes of *mutual* and *reciprocal* interest are not realized. We do not know how much interest she has in him by the end of their time together, but whatever her feelings she comes under pressure to have sex with him,

and she does not want to have the kind of sex he wants. She may desire to hold hands and kiss, to engage in more intense caresses or in some form of foreplay, or she may not want to be touched. She may have reasons unrelated to desire for not wanting to engage in the kind of sex he is demanding. She may have religious reservations, concerns about pregnancy or disease, a disinclination to be just another conquest. She may be engaged in a seduction program of her own which sees abstaining from sexual activity as a means of building an important emotional bond. She feels she is desirable to him, and she knows and he knows that he will have sex with her if he can. And while she feels she doesn't owe him anything and that it is her prerogative to refuse him, this feeling is partly a defensive reaction against a deeply held belief that if he is in need she should provide. If she buys into the myth of insistent male sexuality, she may feel he is suffering from sexual frustration and that she is largely to blame.

We do not know how much he desires her, but we do know that his desire for erotic satisfaction can hardly be separated from his desire for conquest. He feels no dating obligation, but has a strong commitment to scoring. He uses the myth of "so hard to control" male desire as a rhetorical tactic, telling her how frustrated she will leave him. He becomes overbearing. She resists, voicing her disinclination. He alternates between telling her how desirable she is and taking a hostile stance, charging her with misleading him, accusing her of wanting him, and being coy—in short, of being deceitful, all the time engaging in rather aggressive body contact. It is late at night, she is tired and a bit queasy from too many drinks, and he is reaffirming her suspicion that perhaps she has misled him. She is having trouble disengaging his body from hers, and wishes he would just go away. She does not adopt a strident angry stance, partly because she thinks he is acting normally and does not deserve it, partly because she feels she is partly to blame, and partly because there is always the danger that her anger will make him angry, possibly violent. It seems that the only thing to do, given his aggression and her queasy fatigue, is to go along with him and get it over with, but this decision is so entangled with the events in process it is hard to know if it is not simply a recognition of what is actually happening. She finds the whole encounter a thoroughly disagreeable experience, but he does not take any notice and wouldn't have changed course if he had. He congratulates himself on his sexual prowess and is confirmed in his opinion that aggressive tactics pay off. Later she feels that she has been raped but, paradoxically, tells herself that she let herself be raped.

The paradoxical feelings of the woman in our example indicate her awareness that what she feels about the incident stands in contradiction to the prevailing cultural assessment of it. She knows that she did not want to have sex with her date. She is not so sure, however, about how much her own desires count, and she is uncertain that she has made her desires clear. Her uncertainty is reinforced by the cultural reading of this incident as an ordinary seduction.

As for us, we assume that the woman did not want to have sex, but just like her, we are unsure whether her mere reluctance, in the presence of high-pressure tactics, constitutes nonconsent. We suspect that submission to an overbearing and insensitive lout is no way to go about attaining sexual enjoyment, and we further suspect that he felt no compunction about providing it, so that on the face of it, from the outside looking in, it looks like a pretty unreasonable proposition for her.

Let us look at this reasoning more closely. Assume that she was not attracted to the kind of sex offered by the sort of person offering it. Then it would be *prima facie* unreasonable for her to agree to have sex—unreasonable, that is, unless she were offered some payoff for her stoic endurance, money perhaps, or tickets to the opera. The reason is that in sexual matters agreement is closely connected to attraction. Thus, where the presumption is that she was not attracted, we should at the same time presume that she did not consent. Hence, the burden of proof should be on her alleged assailant to show that she had good reasons for consenting to an unattractive proposition.

This is not, however, the way such situations are interpreted. In the unlikely event that the example I have described should come before the courts, there is little doubt that the law would interpret the woman's eventual acquiescence or "going along with" the sexual encounter as consent. But along with this interpretation would go the implicit understanding that she had consented because when all was said and done, when the "token" resistances to the "masterful advances" had been made, she had wanted to after all. Once the courts have constructed this interpretation, they are then forced to conjure up some horror story of feminine revenge in order to explain why she should bring charges against her "seducer."

In the even more unlikely event that the courts agreed that the woman had not consented to the above encounter, there is little chance that her assailant would be convicted of sexual assault.[11] The belief that the man's aggressive tactics are a normal part of seduction means that *mens rea* cannot be established. Her eventual "going along" with his advances constitutes reasonable grounds for his believing in her consent. These "reasonable" grounds attest to the sincerity of his belief in her consent. This reasonableness means that *mens rea* would be defeated even in jurisdictions which make *mens rea* a function of objective standards of reasonableness. Moreover, the sympathy of the court is more likely to lie with the rapist than with his victim, since, if the court is typical, it will be strongly inclined to believe that the victim had in some way "asked for it."

The position of the courts is supported by the widespread belief that male aggression and female reluctance are normal parts of seduction. Given their acceptance of this model, the logic of their response must be respected. For if sexual aggression is a part of ordinary seduction, then it cannot be inconsistent with the legitimate consent of the person allegedly seduced by this means. And if it is normal for a woman to be reluctant, then this reluctance must be consistent with her consent as well. The position of the courts is not inconsistent just so long as they allow that some sort of protest on the part of a woman counts as a refusal. As we have seen, however, it frequently happens that no sort of protest would count as a refusal. Moreover, if no sort of protest counts, or at least if precious few count, then the failure to register these protests will amount to "asking for it," will amount, in other words, to agreeing.

The court's belief in "natural" male aggression and "natural" female reluctance has increasingly come under attack by feminist critics who see quite correctly that the entire legal position would collapse if, for example, it were shown empirically that men were not aggressive and that women, at least when they wanted sex, were. This strategy is of little help, however, so long as aggressive men can still be found and relics of reluctant women continue to

11. See Jeanne C. Marsh, Allison Geist, and Nathan Caplan, *Rape and the Limits of Law Reform* (Boston: Auburn House, 1982), 32. According to Marsh's study on the impact of the Michigan reform of rape laws, convictions were increased for traditional conceptions of rape, i.e., aggravated assault. However date rape, which has a much higher incidence than aggravated assault, has a very low rate of arrest and an even lower one of conviction.

surface. Fortunately, there is another strategy. The position collapses through the weakness of its internal logic. The next section traces the several lines of this logic.

Rape Myths

The belief that the natural aggression of men and the natural reluctance of women somehow make date rape understandable underlies a number of prevalent myths about rape and human sexuality. These beliefs maintain their force partly on account of a logical compulsion exercised by them at an unconscious level. The only way of refuting them effectively is to excavate the logical propositions involved and to expose their misapplication to the situations to which they have been applied. In what follows, I propose to excavate the logical support for popular attitudes that are tolerant of date rape. These myths are not just popular, however, but often emerge in the arguments of judges who acquit date rapists, and of policemen who refuse to lay charges.

The claim that the victim provoked a sexual incident, that "she asked for it," is by far the most common defense given by men who are accused of sexual assault.[12] Feminists, rightly incensed by this response, often treat it as beneath contempt, singling out the defense as an argument against it. On other fronts, sociologists have identified the response as part of an overall tendency of people to see the world as just, a tendency which disposes them to conclude that people for the most part deserve what they get.[13] However, an inclination to see the world as just requires us to construct an account which yields this outcome, and it is just such an account that I wish to examine with regard to date rape.

12. See ibid., 61, for a particularly good example of this response. Also see John M. MacDonald, "Victim-Precipitated Rape," in *Rape Offenders and Their Victims* (Springfield, Ill.: Charles C. Thomas, 1971), 78–89, for a good example of this response in academic thinking. Also see Menachem Amir, *Patterns in Forcible Rape* (Chicago: University of Chicago Press, 1972), 259.

13. See Eugene Borgida and Nancy Brekke, "Psycholegal Research on Rape Trials," in *Rape and Sexual Assault,* ed. Ann Wobert Burgess (New York: Garland Press, 1985), 314. Also see M. J. Lerner, "The Desire for Justice and Reactions to Victims," in *Altruism and Helping Behaviour,* ed. J. Macaulay and L. Berkowitz (New York: Academic Press, 1970).

The least sophisticated of the "she asked for it" rationales—and in a sense, the easiest to deal with—appeals to an injunction against sexually provocative behavior on the part of women. If women should not be sexually provocative, then, from this standpoint, a woman who is sexually provocative deserves to suffer the consequences. Now it will not do to respond that women get raped even when they are not sexually provocative, or that it is men who get to interpret (unfairly) what counts as sexually provocative.[14] The question should be: Why shouldn't a woman be sexually provocative? Why should this behavior warrant any kind of aggressive response whatsoever?

Attempts to explain that women have a right to behave in sexually provocative ways without suffering dire consequences still meet with surprisingly tough resistance. Even people who find nothing wrong or sinful with sex itself, in any of its forms, tend to suppose that women must not behave sexually unless they are prepared to carry through on some fuller course of sexual interaction. The logic of this response seems to be that at some point a woman's behavior commits her to following through on the full course of a sexual encounter as it is defined by her assailant. At some point she has made an agreement, or formed a contract, and once that is done, her contractor is entitled to demand that she satisfy the terms of that contract. Thus, this view about sexual responsibility and desert is supported by other assumptions about contracts and agreements. But we do not normally suppose that casual nonverbal behavior generates agreements. Nor do we normally grant private persons the right to enforce contracts. What rationale would support our conclusion in this case?

The rationale, I believe, comes in the form of a belief in the especially insistent nature of male sexuality, an insistence which lies at the root of natural male aggression and which is extremely difficult, perhaps impossible, to contain. At a certain point in the arousal process, it is thought, a man's rational will gives way to the prerogatives of nature. His sexual need can and does reach a point where it is uncontrollable, and his natural masculine aggression kicks in to ensure that this need is met. Women, however, are naturally more contained, and so it is their responsibility not to

14. As, for example, Lorenne Clark and Debra Lewis do in *Rape: The Price of Coercive Sexuality* (Toronto: Women's Press, 1977), 152–53.

provoke the irrational in the male. If they do go so far as that, they have both failed in their responsibilities and subjected themselves to the inevitable. One does not go into the lion's cage and expect not to be eaten. Natural feminine reluctance, it is thought, is no protection against a sexually aroused male.

This belief about the normal aggressiveness of male sexuality is complemented by common knowledge about female gender development. Once, women were taught to deny their sexuality and to aspire to ideals of chastity. Things have not changed so much. Women still tend to eschew conquest mentalities in favor of a combination of sex and affection. Insofar as this is thought to be merely a cultural requirement, however, there is an expectation that women will be coy about their sexual desire. The assumption that women both want to indulge sexually and are inclined to sacrifice this desire for higher ends, gives rise to the myth that they want to be raped. After all, doesn't rape give them the sexual enjoyment they *really* want, at the same time that it relieves them of the responsibility for admitting to and acting upon what they want? And how then can we blame men, who have been socialized to be aggressively seductive precisely for the purpose of overriding female reserve? If we find fault at all, we are inclined to cast our suspicions on the motives of the woman. For it is on her that the contradictory roles of sexual desirer and sexual denier have been placed. Our awareness of the contradiction expected of her makes us suspect her honesty. In the past, she was expected to deny her complicity because of the shame and guilt she felt at having submitted.[15] This expectation persists in many quarters today and is carried over into a general suspicion about her character, and the fear that she might make a false accusation out of revenge or some other low motive.[16]

But if women really want sexual pleasure, what inclines us to think that they will get it through rape? This conclusion logically requires a theory about the dynamics of sexual pleasure that sees that pleasure as an emergent property of overwhelming male insistence. For the assumption that a raped female experiences sexual pleasure implies that the person who rapes her knows how to

15. See Sue Bessner, *The Laws of Rape* (New York: Praeger Publications, 1984), 111–21, for a discussion of the legal forms in which this suspicion is expressed.
16. Ibid.

cause that pleasure independently of any information she might convey on that point. Since her ongoing protest is inconsistent with requests to be touched in particular ways in particular places, to have more of this and less of that, then we must believe that the person who touches her knows these particular ways and places instinctively, without any directives from her.

Thus we find, underlying and reinforcing this belief in incommunicative male prowess, a conception of sexual pleasure that springs from wordless interchanges and of sexual success that occurs in a place of meaningful silence. The language of seduction is accepted as a tacit language: eye contact, smiles, blushes, and faintly discernible gestures. It is, accordingly, imprecise and ambiguous. It would be easy for a man to make mistakes about the message conveyed, understandable that he should mistakenly think that a sexual invitation has been made and a bargain struck. But honest mistakes, we think, must be excused.

In sum, the belief that women should not be sexually provocative is logically linked to several other beliefs, some normative, some empirical. The normative beliefs are (1) that people should keep the agreements they make; (2) that sexually provocative behavior, taken beyond a certain point, generates agreements; (3) that the peculiar nature of male and female sexuality places such agreements in a special category, one in which the possibility of retracting an agreement is ruled out or at least made highly unlikely; (4) that women are not to be trusted, in sexual matters at least. The empirical belief, which turns out to be false, is that male sexuality is not subject to rational and moral control.

Dispelling the Myths

The "she asked for it" justification of sexual assault incorporates a conception of a contract that would be difficult to defend in any other context, and the presumptions about human sexuality which function to reinforce sympathies rooted in the contractual notion of just deserts are not supported by empirical research.

The belief that a woman generates some sort of contractual obligation whenever her behavior is interpreted as seductive is the most indefensible part of the mythology of rape. In law, contracts are not legitimate just because a promise has been made. In particular, the use of pressure tactics to extract agreement is frowned upon. Normally, an agreement is upheld only if the contractors were clear on what they were getting into and had sufficient time to reflect on the wisdom of their doing so. Either there must be a clear tradition in which the expectations involved in the contract are fairly well known (marriage), or there must be an explicit written agreement concerning the exact terms of the contract and the expectations of the persons involved. But whatever the terms of a contract, there is no private right to enforce it. So, if I make a contract with you on which I renege, the only permissible recourse for you is through due legal process.

Now, it is not clear whether sexual contracts can be made to begin with or, if so, what sort of sexual contracts would be legitimate. But assuming that they could be made, the terms of those contracts would not be enforceable. To allow public enforcement would be to grant the state the overt right to force people to have sex, and this would clearly be unacceptable. Granting that sexual contracts are legitimate, state enforcement of such contracts would have to be limited to ordering nonsexual compensation for breaches of contract. So it makes no difference whether a sexual contract is tacit or explicit. There are no grounds whatsoever that would justify enforcement of its terms.

Thus, even if we assume that a woman has initially agreed to an encounter, her agreement does not automatically make all subsequent sexual activity to which she submits legitimate. If during coitus a woman should experience pain, be suddenly overcome with guilt or fear of pregnancy, or simply lose her initial desire, those are good reasons for her to change her mind. Having changed her mind, neither her partner nor the state has any right to force her to continue. But then if she is forced to continue she is assaulted. Thus, establishing that consent occurred at a particular point during a sexual encounter should not conclusively establish the legitimacy of the encounter.[17] What is needed is a reading of whether she agreed throughout the encounter.

17. A speech-act like "OK, let's get it over with" is taken as consent, even though it is extracted under high pressure, the sex that ensues lacks mutuality, and there are no ulterior reasons for such an agreement. See Davis, "Setting Penalties," 103. Also see Carolyn Schafer and Marilyn Frye, "Rape and Respect," in *Readings in Recent Feminist Philosophy,* ed. Marilyn Pearsall (Belmont, Calif.: Wadsworth, 1986), 189, for a characterization of the common notion of consent as a formal speech-act.

If the "she asked for it" contractual view of sexual interchange has any validity, it is because there is a point at which there is no stopping a sexual encounter, a point at which that encounter becomes the inexorable outcome of the unfolding of natural events. If a sexual encounter is like a slide on which I cannot stop halfway down, it will be relevant whether I enter the slide of my own free will or am pushed.

But there is no evidence that the entire sexual act is like a slide. While there may be a few seconds in the "plateau" period just prior to orgasm in which people are "swept" away by sexual feelings to the point where we could justifiably understand their lack of heed for the comfort of their partner, the greater part of a sexual encounter comes well within the bounds of morally responsible control of our own actions. Indeed, the available evidence shows that most of the activity involved in sex has to do with building the requisite level of desire, a task that involves the proper use of foreplay, the possibility of which implies control over the form that foreplay will take. Modern sexual therapy assumes that such control is universally accessible, and so far there has been no reason to question that assumption. Sexologists are unanimous, moreover, in holding that mutual sexual enjoyment requires an atmosphere of comfort and communication, a minimum of pressure, and an ongoing checkup on one's partner's state. They maintain that different people have different predilections and that what is pleasurable for one person is very often anathema to another. These findings show that the way to achieve sexual pleasure, at any time at all, let alone with a casual acquaintance, decidedly does not involve overriding the other person's express reservations and providing them with just any kind of sexual stimulus.[18] And while we do not want to allow science and technology a voice in which the voices of particular women are drowned, in this case

18. It is not just women who fail to find satisfaction in the "swept away" approach to sexual interaction. Studies of convicted rapists, and of conquest-oriented men, indicate that men are frequently disappointed when they use this approach as well. In over half of aggravated sexual assaults, penetration fails because the man loses his erection. Those who do succeed invariably report that the sex experienced was not enjoyable. This supports the prevailing view of sexologists that men depend on the positive response of their partners in order to fuel their own responsive mechanisms. See A. N. Groth, in *Rape and Sexual Assault*. Also see *Why Men Rape*, ed. Levine and Koenig, or consult any recent manual on male sexuality.

science seems to concur with women's perception that aggressive incommunicative sex is not what they want. But if science and the voice of women concur, if aggressive seduction does not lead to good sex, if women do not like it or want it, then it is not rational to think that they would agree to it. Where such sex takes place, it is therefore rational to presume that the sex was not consensual.

The myth that women like to be raped is closely connected, as we have seen, to doubt about their honesty in sexual matters, and this suspicion is exploited by defense lawyers when sexual assault cases make it to the courtroom. It is an unfortunate consequence of the presumption of innocence that rape victims who end up in court frequently find that it is they who are on trial. For if the defendant is innocent, then either he did not intend to do what he was accused of, or the plaintiff is mistaken about his identity, or she is lying. Often the last alternative is the only plausible defense, and as a result the plaintiff's word seldom goes unquestioned. Women are frequently accused of having made a false accusation, either as a defensive mechanism for dealing with guilt and shame or out of a desire for revenge.

Now, there is no point in denying the possibility of false accusation, though there are probably better ways of seeking revenge on a man than accusing him of rape. However, we can now establish a logical connection between the evidence that a woman was subjected to high-pressure aggressive "seduction" tactics and her claim that she did not consent to that encounter. Where the kind of encounter is not the sort to which it would be reasonable to consent, there is a logical presumption that a woman who claims she did not consent is telling the truth. Where the kind of sex involved is not the sort of sex we would expect a woman to like, the burden of proof should be not on the woman to show that she did not consent but on the defendant to show that, contrary to every reasonable expectation, she did consent. The defendant should be required to convince the court that the plaintiff persuaded him to have sex with her even though there are no visible reasons why she should.

In conclusion, there are no grounds for the "she asked for it" defense. Sexually provocative behavior does not generate sexual contracts. Even where there are sexual agreements, they cannot be legitimately enforced by the state or by private right or by natural prerogative. Second, all the evidence suggests that neither women nor men find sexual enjoyment in rape or in any form of noncommunicative sexuality. Third, male sexual desire is containable and can be subjected to moral and rational control. Fourth, since there is no reason why women should not be sexually provocative, they do not "deserve" any sex they do not want. This last is a welcome discovery. The taboo on sexual provocativeness in women is a taboo both on sensuality and on teasing. But sensuality is a source of delight, and teasing is playful and inspires wit. What a relief to learn that it is not sexual provocativeness, but its enemies, that constitutes a danger to the world.

Communicative Sexuality: Reinterpreting the Kantian Imperative

The present criterion of consent sets up sexual encounters as contractual events in which sexual aggression is presumed to be consented to unless there is some vigorous act of refusal. As long as we view sexual interaction on a contractual model, the only possibility for finding fault is to point to the presence of such an act. But it is clear that whether or not we can determine such a presence, there is something strongly disagreeable about the sexual aggression described above.

In thinking about sex we must keep in mind its sensual ends, and the facts show that aggressive high-pressure sex contradicts those ends. Consensual sex in dating situations is presumed to aim at mutual enjoyment. It may not always do this, and when it does, it might not always succeed. There is no logical incompatibility between wanting to continue a sexual encounter and failing to derive sexual pleasure from it.[19]

But it seems to me that there is a presumption in favor of the connection between sex and sexual enjoyment, and that if a man wants to be sure he is not forcing himself on a woman he has an obligation either to ensure that the encounter really is mutually

---

19. Robin Morgan comes perilously close to suggesting that there is when she defines rape as any sexual encounter that is not initiated by a woman out of her own heartfelt desire. See *Going Too Far* (New York: Random House, 1968), 165.

enjoyable or to know the reasons why she would want to continue the encounter in spite of her lack of enjoyment. A closer investigation of the nature of this obligation will enable us to construct a more rational and a more plausible norm of sexual conduct.

Onora O'Neill has argued that in intimate situations we have an obligation to take the ends of others as our own and to promote those ends in a nonmanipulative and nonpaternalistic manner.[20] Now, it seems that in honest sexual encounters just this is required. Assuming that each person enters the encounter in order to seek sexual satisfaction, each person engaging in the encounter has an obligation to help the other seek his or her ends. To do otherwise is to risk acting in opposition to what the other desires, and hence to risk acting without the other's consent.

But the obligation to promote the sexual ends of one's partner implies the obligation to know what those ends are, and also the obligation to know how those ends are attained. Thus, the problem comes down to a problem of epistemic responsibility, the responsibility to know. The solution, in my view, lies in the practice of a communicative sexuality, one which combines the appropriate knowledge of the other with respect for the dialectics of desire.

So let us, for a moment, conceive of sexual interaction on a communicative rather than contractual model. Let us look at it the way I think it should be looked at, as if it were a proper conversation rather than an offer from the Mafia.

Conversations, when they are proper conversations as opposed to lectures, diatribes, or interrogations, illustrate the logical relation between communicative interaction and treating someone as an end in herself in O'Neill's sense. This logical relation can be illustrated by the difference in kind between a typical contract and a proper sort of conversation, a difference that derives primarily from the different relation each bears to the necessity for cooperation. The difference is this: typically, where contracts are concerned, cooperation is primarily required as a means to some further end set by the contract. In proper conversations, as I shall define them here, cooperation is sought as an end in itself.

It is not inimical to most contracts that the cooperation necessary for achieving its ends be reluctant or even hostile. Although

20. O'Neill, "Between Consenting Adults," *Philosophy and Public Affairs* 14:252–77.

we can find fault with a contractor for failing to deliver goods or services, we do not normally criticize her for her attitude. And although there are situations where we employ people on the condition that they be congenial, even then we do not require that their congeniality be the real thing. When we are having a proper conversation, however, we do, typically, want the real thing. In conversation, the cooperation with the other is not just a means to an interesting conversation; it is one of the ends we seek, without which the conversation ceases to satisfy.

The communicative interaction involved in conversation is concerned with a good deal more than didactic content and argument. Good conversationalists are intuitive, sympathetic, and charitable. Intuition and charity aid the conversationalist in her effort to interpret the words of the other correctly, and sympathy enables her to enter into the other's point of view. Her sensitivity alerts her to the tone of the exchange. Has her point been taken good-humoredly or resentfully? Aggressively delivered responses are taken as a sign that *ad hominems* are at work and that the respondent's self-worth has been called into question. Good conversationalists will know to suspend further discussion until this sense of self-worth has been reestablished. Angry responses, resentful responses, bored responses, even overenthusiastic responses require that the emotional ground be cleared before the discussion be continued. Often it is better to change the topic or to come back to it another day under different circumstances. Good conversationalists do not overwhelm their respondents with a barrage of their own opinions. While they may be persuasive, the forcefulness of their persuasion does not lie in their being overbearing, but rather in their capacity to see the other's point of view, to understand what it depends on, and so to address the essential point, but with tact and clarity.

Just as communicative conversationalists are concerned with more than didactic content, persons engaged in communicative sexuality will be concerned with more than achieving coitus. They will be sensitive to the responses of their partners. They will, like good conversationalists, be intuitive, sympathetic, and charitable. Intuition will help them to interpret their partner's responses; sympathy will enable them to share what their partner is feeling; charity will enable them to care. Communicative sexual partners will not overwhelm each other with the barrage of their own desires. They will treat negative, bored, or angry responses as a sign that the erotic ground needs to be either cleared or abandoned. Their concern with fostering the desire of the other must involve an ongoing state of alertness in interpreting her responses.

Just as a conversationalist's prime concern is for the mutuality of the discussion, a person engaged in communicative sexuality will be most concerned with the mutuality of desire. As such, both will put into practice a regard for their respondent that is guaranteed no place in the contractual language of rights, duties, and consent. The dialectics of both activities reflect the dialectics of desire insofar as each person's interest in continuing is contingent upon the other person's wishing to do so too, and each person's interest is as much fueled by the other's interest as it is by her own. Each respects the subjectivity of the other not just by avoiding treading on it but by fostering and protecting the quality of that subjectivity. Indeed, the requirement to avoid treading on the subjectivity of the other entails the obligation to respect the dialectics of desire.[21] For in intimacy there is no passing by on the other side. To be intimate just is to open up in emotional and personal ways, to share personal knowledge, and to be receptive to the openness of the other. This openness and sharing normally takes place only in an atmosphere of confidence and trust. But once availed of this knowledge and confidence and trust, one has, as it were, thrust upon one the responsibility not to betray the trust by misusing the knowledge. And only by respecting the dialectics of desire can we have any confidence that we have not misused our position of trust and knowledge.

Cultural Presumptions

Now it may well be that we have no obligation to care for strangers, and I do not wish to claim that we do. Nonetheless, it seems that O'Neill's point about the special moral duties we have in certain

---

21. The sort of relationship I have in mind exemplifies the "feminist" approach to ethics argued for by Nell Noddings, *Caring: A Feminine Approach to Ethics* (Berkeley and Los Angeles: University of California Press, 1984). In particular, see her discussion of teaching as a "duality" (ibid., 195).

intimate situations is supported by a conceptual relation between certain kinds of personal relationships and the expectation that it should be a communicative relation. Friendship is a case in point. It is a relation that is greatly underdetermined by what we usually include in our sets of rights and obligations. For the most part, rights and obligations disappear as terms by which friendship is guided. They are still there, to be called upon, in case the relationship breaks down, but insofar as the friendship is a friendship it is concerned with fostering the quality of the interaction and not with standing on rights. Thus, because we are friends we share our property, and property rights between us are not invoked. Because we are friends, privacy is not an issue. Because we are friends we may see to each other's needs as often as we see to our own. The same can be said for relations between lovers, parents, and dependent children and even between spouses, at least when interaction is functioning at an optimal level. When such relations break down to the point that people must stand on their rights, we can often say that the actors ought to make more of an effort, and in many instances fault them for their lack of charity, tolerance, or benevolence. Thus, although we have a right to end friendships, it may be a reflection on our lack of virtue that we do so, and while we cannot be criticized for violating other people's rights, we can be rightfully deprecated for lacking the virtue to sustain a friendship.

But is there a similar conceptual relation between the kind of activity that a date is and the sort of moral practice that it requires? My claim is that there is and that this connection is easily established once we recognize the cultural presumption that dating is a gesture of friendship and regard. Traditionally, the decision to date indicates that two people have an initial attraction to each other, that they are disposed to like each other and look forward to enjoying each other's company. Dating derives its implicit meaning from this tradition. It retains this meaning unless other aims are explicitly stated, and even then it may not be possible to alienate this meaning. It is a rare woman who will not spurn a man who states explicitly, right at the onset, that he wants to go out with her solely on the condition that he have sexual intercourse with her at the end of the evening, and that he has no interest in her company apart from gaining that end, and no concern for mutual satisfaction.

Explicit protest to the contrary aside, the conventions of dating confer on it its social meaning, and this social meaning implies a relationship which is more like friendship than the cutthroat competition of opposing teams. As such, it requires that we do more than stand on our rights with regard to each other. As long as we are operating under the auspices of a dating relationship, it requires that we behave in the mode of friendship and trust. But if a date is more like a friendship than a business contract, then clearly respect for the dialectics of desire is incompatible with the sort of sexual pressure that is inclined to end in date rape. And clearly, also, a conquest mentality which exploits a situation of trust and respect for purely selfish ends is morally pernicious. Failure to respect the dialectics of desire when operating under the auspices of friendship and trust is to act in flagrant disregard of the moral requirement to avoid manipulative, coercive, and exploitive behavior. Respect for the dialectics of desire is *prima facie* inconsistent with the satisfaction of one person at the expense of the other. The proper end of friendship relations is mutual satisfaction. But the requirement of mutuality means that we must take a communicative approach to discovering the ends of the other, and this entails that we respect the dialectics of desire.

But now that we know what communicative sexuality is, and that it is morally required, and that it is the only feasible means to mutual sexual enjoyment, why not take this model as the norm of what is reasonable in sexual interaction? The evidence of sexologists strongly indicates that women whose partners are aggressively uncommunicative have little chance of experiencing sexual pleasure. But it is not reasonable for women to consent to what they have little chance of enjoying. Hence, it is not reasonable for women to consent to aggressive noncommunicative sex. Nor can we reasonably suppose that women have consented to sexual encounters which we know and they know they do not find enjoyable. With the communicative model as the norm, the aggressive contractual model should strike us as a model of deviant sexuality, and sexual encounters patterned on that model should strike us as encounters to which *prima facie* no one would reasonably agree. But if acquiescence to an encounter counts as consent only if the acquiescence is reasonable, something to which a reasonable person, in full possession of knowledge relevant to the encounter, would agree, then acquiescence to aggressive noncommunicative sex is not reasonable. Hence, acquiescence under such conditions should not count as consent.

Thus, where communicative sexuality does not occur, we lack the main ground for believing that the sex involved was consensual. Moreover, where a man does not engage in communicative sexuality, he acts either out of reckless disregard or out of willful ignorance, for he cannot know, except through the practice of communicative sexuality, whether his partner has any sexual reason for continuing the encounter. And where she does not, he runs the risk of imposing on her what she is not willing to have. All that is needed, then, in order to provide women with legal protection from "date rape" is to make both reckless indifference and willful ignorance a sufficient condition of *mens rea* and to make communicative sexuality the accepted norm of sex to which a reasonable woman would agree.[22] Thus, the appeal to communicative sexuality as a norm for sexual encounters accomplishes two things. It brings the aggressive sex involved in "date rape" well within the realm of sexual assault, and it locates the guilt of date-rapists in the failure to approach sexual relations on a communicative basis.

The Epistemological Implications

Finding a proper criterion for consent is one problem, but discovering what really happened, after the event, when the only eyewitnesses give conflicting accounts, is another. But while there is no foolproof way of getting the unadulterated truth, it can make a significant difference to the outcome of a prosecution the sort of facts we are seeking. On the old model of aggressive seduction, we sought evidence of resistance. But on the new model of communicative sexuality, what we want is evidence of an ongoing positive and encouraging response on the part of the plaintiff. This new goal will require quite different tactics on the part of the cross-examiners, and quite different expectations on the part of juries and judges. Where communicative sexuality is taken as the norm, and aggressive sexual tactics as a presumption against consent, the

---

22. As now seems to be the case in Australian law. See note 4 above.

outcome for the example I described above would be quite different. It would be regarded as sexual assault rather than seduction.

Let us then consider a date rape trial in which a man is cross-examined. He is asked whether he was presuming mutual sexual enjoyment. Suppose he answers in the negative. Then he would have to account for why he persisted in the face of her voiced reluctance. He cannot give as an excuse that he thought she liked it, because he believes that she did not. If he thought that she had consented even though she didn't like it, then it seems to me that the burden of proof would lie with him to say why it was reasonable to think this. Clearly, her initial resistance, her presumed lack of enjoyment, and the pressure tactics involved in getting her to "go along" would not support a reasonable belief in consent, and his persisting in the face of her dissatisfaction would surely cast doubt on the sincerity of his belief in her consent.

But suppose he answers in the affirmative. Then the cross-examiner would not have to rely on the old criteria for nonconsent. He would not have to show either that she had resisted him or that she was in a fearful or intimidated state of mind. Instead, he could use a communicative model of sexuality to discover how much respect there had been for the dialectics of desire. Did he ask her what she liked? If she was using contraceptives? If he should? What tone of voice did he use? How did she answer? Did she make any demands? Did she ask for penetration? How was that desire conveyed? Did he ever let up the pressure long enough to see if she was really that interested? Did he ask her which position she preferred? Assuming that the defendant does not perjure himself, he would lack satisfactory answers to these questions. But even where the defendant did lie, a skilled cross-examiner who was willing to go into detail could probably establish easily enough when the interaction had not been communicative. It is extraordinarily difficult to keep up a consistent story when you are not telling the truth.

On the new criterion, the cross-examination focuses on the communicative nature of the ongoing encounter, and the communicative nature of an encounter is much easier to establish than the occurrence of an episodic act of resistance. For one thing, it requires that a fairly long yet consistent story be told, and this enables us to assess the plausibility of the competing claims in light of a wider collection of relevant data. Second, in making noncommunicative sex the primary indicator of coercive sex, it provides us with a criterion for distinguishing consensual sadomasochism from brutality. For even if a couple agree to sadomasochistic sex—bondage and whippings and the rest of it—the court has a right to require that there be a system of signals whereby each partner can convey to the other whether she has had enough.[23] Third, the use of a new criterion of communicative sexuality would enable us to introduce a new category of nonaggravated sexual assault which would not necessarily carry a heavy sentence but which would nonetheless provide an effective recourse against "date rape."[24]

Conclusion

In sum, using communicative sexuality as a model of normal sex has several advantages over the "aggressive-acquiescence" model of seduction. The new model ties the presumption that consensual sex takes place in the expectation of mutual desire much more closely to the facts about how that desire actually functions. Where communicative sex does not occur, this establishes a presumption that there was no consent. The importance of this presumption is that we are able, in criminal proceedings, to shift the burden of proof from the plaintiff, who on the contractual model must show that she resisted or was threatened, to the defendant, who must then give some reason why she should consent after all. The communicative model of sexuality also enables us to give a different conceptual content to the concept of consent. It sees consent as something more like an ongoing cooperation than the one-shot agreement which we are inclined to see it as on the contractual model. Moreover, it does not matter, on the communicative model, whether a woman was sexually provocative, what her reputation

---

23. The SAMOIS justification of sadomasochism rests on the claim that sadomasochistic practice can be communicative in this way. See SAMOIS, *Coming to Power* (Boston: Alyson Publication, 1981).

24. See Sections 520e, Act No. 266, State of Michigan. Sexual assault in the fourth degree is punishable by imprisonment of not more than two years or a fine of not more than $500, or both.

is, what went on before the sex began. All that matters is the quality of communication with regard to the sex itself.

But most important, the communicative model of normal sexuality gives us a handle on a solution to the problem of date rape. If noncommunicative sexuality establishes a presumption of nonconsent, then where there are no overriding reasons for thinking that consent occurred we have a criterion for a category of sexual assault that does not require evidence of physical violence or threat. If we are serious about date rape, then the next step is to take this criterion as objective grounds for establishing that a date rape has occurred. The proper legislation is the shortest route to establishing this criterion.

There remains, of course, the problem of education. If we are going to change the rules about what is socially acceptable in sexual relations, then it is only fair to let the public know. In a mass-media society, this is not hard to do. A public information campaign will spread the news in no time at all. The real problem is the reluctance of the mass media to deal with questions of sexual relations and sexual intimacy. Its politicians are still curiously reluctant to stand up to an increasingly small sector of society that is unwilling to admit, despite all the evidence to the contrary, that anyone but well-meaning husbands and wives ever have sex. I would not be surprised if this sort of puritanical holdout were the very source of the problem of rape. Certainly, sexual ignorance must contribute significantly to the kind of social environment conducive to rape.

2

Date Rape and Erotic Discourse

David M. Adams

Lois Pineau has taken a significant step in the right direction toward a reconceptualization of rape doctrine, a part of the law badly in need of all the help it can get.[1] While in substantial agreement with the core of Pineau's argument, I do believe we should be mindful of the limitations of her revised model of reasonableness in rape law. I therefore offer the following comments *ex abundanti cautela.*

Pineau is concerned with what has come to be called date rape or acquaintance rape: cases of nonaggravated sexual assault, absent any showing of an injury to the victim (such as a beating) or a threat of injury and where the persons involved are nonstrangers.

---

1. Lois Pineau, "Date Rape: A Feminist Analysis," *Law and Philosophy* 8 (1989), 217–43. This article is reprinted as Chapter 1 of this book.

The problem posed by this form of sexual assault is that, however deeply violative of the victim's person, date rape is rarely if ever found by judge or jury to be real rape. Under the standard doctrinal approach, the offense of nonaggravated sexual assault requires (1) nonconsensual sexual relations coupled with (2), at a minimum, an unreasonable belief in the consent of the victim. Pineau, along with other feminist theorists, argues that the law's working understanding of nonaggravated sexual assault is deeply embedded within an ideology which sees male aggression and female reluctance, conquest and submission, as the norm through which all sexual encounters are to be assessed. This is most clearly evident in the substantive and evidentiary issues bearing on the question of consent.

As Susan Estrich has carefully documented,[2] both traditional common law and modern doctrine approach the question of whether an act of sex was consensual by looking either for evidence (on the part of the victim) of demonstrated resistance or of failure to resist due to fear of bodily injury, or (on the part of the defendant) of the use of force. Such an approach is tantamount, as both Pineau and Estrich observe, to setting up a presumption of consent to sexual encounters, a presumption then to be defeated (if possible) through introduction of evidence showing resistance or use of force. But the assumptions about women, men, and sexuality within which the law of rape is located make it virtually impossible for the female victim of a nonaggravated sexual encounter to produce evidence sufficient to establish that assault.

What counts as resistance or force, what is understood to be a threat, what is taken to be unreasonable about a belief—all are substantially if not entirely *gendered:* they are conceived (in the case of existing legal doctrine) from a male point of view and reflect distorted images of women and of sexuality. As Estrich argues, the courts, for example, typically view the force/resistance polarity on the model of the schoolboy fight on the playground;[3] hence, a man who procured sex from a woman by impassively informing her that he would "fix her face" if she didn't submit was acquitted because he used no "force," since brandishing of fists and use of muscles was not necessary to accomplish his objective (nor did

2. Estrich, *Real Rape.*
3. Ibid., chap. 4.

she raise fists to resist).[4] The widely discussed *Rusk*[5] case from the early 1980s drives home the same point. The defendant met his victim at a bar and asked her for a ride home. She agreed. When they arrived it was late at night in a neighborhood unfamiliar to the woman. He asked her up to his apartment; she refused. He asked again. Upon her second refusal, he reached over and took her car keys. She accompanied him upstairs, where he pulled her by the arms onto the bed and began to undress her. Crying, she testified: "I was really scared, because I can't describe, you know, what was said. It was more the look in his eyes, . . . and I said 'If I do what you want, will you let me go without killing me?' . . . He said yes and I proceeded to do what he wanted me to."[6] Though ultimately his conviction was sustained, many of the judges hearing this case found, in the words of one judge, "no conduct by the defendant reasonably calculated to make the victim so fearful that she should fail to resist."[7] No force was employed; the victim's alleged fear sprang from nothing of substance. In this view, the defendant committed no rape but a seduction; his belief that she "went along with it" was not unreasonable from *his* point of view. Courts have also been reluctant to allow rape convictions to stand where the defendant and the victim have had a recognized or prior relationship of some kind—whether they are neighbors, friends, or partners on a date, and especially where they have had a prior intimate relationship.[8]

All of this has been supported by and further reinforced a range of false and pernicious assumptions about women and sex: that women who are raped "ask for it" through their own "contributory behavior"; that women should not be sexually assertive unless they are prepared to carry through; that provocative conduct cre-

---

4. *State v. Alston*, 310 N.C. 399, 312 S.E.2d 470 (1984).

5. 289 Md. 230, 424 A.2d 720 (1981).

6. Ibid., 722.

7. Ibid., 733 (Cole, J., dissenting). The dissent further observes: "She also testified that she was afraid of 'the way he looked,' and afraid of his statement, 'come on up, come on up.' But what can the majority conclude from this statement coupled with a 'look' that remained undescribed? There is no evidence whatsoever to suggest that this was anything other than a pattern of conduct consistent with the ordinary seduction of a female acquaintance who at first suggests her disinclination" (ibid., 733). The majority cites the lower court, finding that " 'the way he looked' fails utterly to support the fear required by [law]" (ibid., 724).

8. See Estrich, *Real Rape*, chap. 2.

ates an implied-in-fact sexual contract or raises male libido to unstoppable levels; that women are vindictive and dishonest, so that fresh complaints and evidence corroborative of allegations made are essentials for conviction.

The great merit of Pineau's article is that it took on the difficult task of framing substantive and evidentiary standards for nonaggravated sexual assault which will overcome the deficits so plainly evident in the standard legal approach. The law, Pineau asserts, should begin with the presumption that consensual sex aims at the mutual enjoyment of the parties. And the best way to secure such mutual satisfaction is through the language of communication and conversation, by participating in and sustaining an erotic discourse. The standard of communicative sexuality centers on the conversational give-and-take of lovers, constituting a "dialectics of desire." Unlike sex on the traditional, "contract" model, in which the parties treat each other's sexuality as a means to ends given independently of their relationship, the model of communicative sexuality conceives of the sexual encounter as a mutually constitutive, cooperative venture, a version of what Alasdair MacIntyre calls a *practice:* an activity or process, the end or good of which is internal to the activity itself.[9] On the traditional model, it is a sufficient condition of consent that the alleged victim either has failed actively to resist or that she was not prevented from putting up such resistance by threats of immediate bodily harm. The inquiry into the defendant's state of mind is thus defined in terms of *indicia* of nonconsent discernible in the victim's conduct; her conduct becomes the focus. Did she resist? If so, how much and in what ways? If not, why not? Did she have good reasons for not resisting? The communicative model seeks to shift the inquiry from such *indicia* of nonconsent to *indicia* of mutuality: What did the defendant do to ascertain the mutuality of the encounter?

Pineau argues that sex which is aggressive and noncommunicative is sex which it would be both unreasonable for a woman to agree to (since she seeks enjoyment and this kind of sex is not enjoyable) and unreasonable for a man to believe she has agreed to (since one should not assume that one's partner consents to what she would not enjoy). Where the evidence shows that the sex is

9. See Alasdair MacIntyre's discussion of practices in *After Virtue,* 2nd ed. (Notre Dame: University of Notre Dame Press, 1984), esp. chap. 4.

not communicative, a presumption of nonconsent is set up, and the burden then shifts to the defendant to show why one could reasonably take his victim to have consented to the sex despite its aggressive, noncommunicative nature. The standard of communicativity thus takes the same basic feature of the situation—the degree of communication which actually took place—as *prima facie* determinative both of the reasonableness of the woman's interest in the sex, and hence of its consensuality, and of the reasonableness of the defendant's belief regarding his victim's willingness. And this means that an aggressive, noncommunicative sexual encounter occurring during a date *is* a genuine form of sexual assault, as dates are social occasions on which there is an expectation of communication and conversation.

What would it mean to consent to sex under the communicative model? We commonly take the giving of consent to something to be a way of defeating the operation of a presumption against the doing of that thing. If you consent to my using your car, this makes sense only against a background assumption that I may not normally do so. Of course, if you consent to my using your car this is not normally understood to be a blanket permission, but rather a permission relative to the context out of which your consent was sought: if I need your car to get my injured child to a hospital, then your consent is understood to extend to the use of the car for that purpose; I may not then proceed to keep the car for a week to run errands. Furthermore, consent normally extends for an implied period of time: if you consent to my using your car for the afternoon, I am free to assume that I need not check back every few minutes to obtain updated permission. Does consent function this way on the model of communicative sexuality? Presumably, on Pineau's model, consent is given incrementally and progressively, a series of acts of consent each tied to the changing context of the situation: consent to be touched, consent to be held, consent to be caressed intimately, and so on.

Taking communicative sexuality to be the standard of reasonableness and consent in the ways outlined, the elements of the offense of nonaggravated sexual assault must then be reconceived, Pineau seems to say, as (1) noncommunicative sexual relations coupled with (2) (minimally) a negligent failure to appreciate the mutuality of the sexual encounter. The communicative model makes it clear that, even though sex is a form of erotic discourse—a mutual, dialectical undertaking—each of the conversationalists has an epistemic responsibility to determine what the other desires, to learn whether he or she wishes to continue and deepen the conversation in particular directions. If either party should fail at this, the communicative model entails, he or she is thereby exposed to liability for noncommunicative sexual assault. The relevant state of mind, then, is one of epistemic irresponsibility: a failure to carry through on one's duty to ensure the mutuality of the encounter. As an empirical matter, of course, it is almost always in our culture the man who fails in this way, and hence it is men who are nearly always charged with rape.

The model of communicative sexuality seems to take as paradigmatic of sexual encounters what might be called authentic sex between Kantian lovers: both participants correctly perceive and weigh their own true desires, and both strive to attain the same degree of clarity with regard to the desires of their partner. Moreover, and as a result of such striving, each demonstrates the fullest measure of respect for the other's sexuality as an end to be furthered rather than as a means to be exploited. The communicative model thus underscores precisely what is most objectionable in the assumptions implicit in traditional rape doctrine: the fact that the reasonableness of the defendant's belief in consent, as well as the reasonableness of the victim's behavior, is consistently measured against male conceptions of force or willingness or resistance shows that the authentic voice of women is being neither heard nor respected.

I would like to raise two general concerns regarding the communicative standard and Pineau's claims for it. The first turns on the extent to which the communicative model embodies the "woman's point of view," the degree to which Pineau's analysis is or ought to be regarded as "feminist." The second involves the defendant's duty of epistemic care, the degree to which a defendant charged with noncommunicative sexual assault can fairly or rightly be held to a high standard of epistemic responsibility. The criterion of communicative sexuality seems to assume that the kind of communication it contemplates has been or can be to a large extent cleansed or purged of what I shall call *gendered* attitudes, beliefs, and conceptual frames. Each of the concerns to which I shall point springs from the suspicion that gendered understandings of sex and sexuality may run deeper than the communicative model can readily accommodate or allow.

Pineau seems to claim that the standard of communicative sexuality expresses both a necessary and a sufficient condition for the reasonableness of a woman's acquiescence in sex. Recent work by some feminist theorists, as I understand it, would challenge both parts of this claim. One line, which I take would be pushed by theorists writing from a more radical feminist stance, says this: While the communicativity of sex may be a necessary condition of its reasonableness, it cannot be a sufficient condition, since the fact that a woman communicates a desire for sex cannot in our culture at least be taken at face value as an authentic report. Catharine MacKinnon, for example, has argued that since the self-definitions and sexual identities of women in our society have been constructed out of experiences of victimization, what they communicate both to themselves and to men about their wants is undercut by the phenomenon of the "false consciousness" of the oppressed—by the extent to which women are unwittingly complicit in their own continued oppression, by the degree to which they trivialize their own pain and humiliation as deserved, view submission as their duty, regard male dominance as somehow natural or inevitable.[10] "The question for social explanation," MacKinnon insists, "becomes not why some women tolerate rape but how any women manage to resent it."[11] Similarly, other theorists, exploring the possibility of a distinctively feminine moral psychology and epistemology, refer to the phenomenon of the "silenced woman": passive, submissive, utterly subordinate to the men in her life, a person both voiceless and selfless;[12] courts in

10. See, generally, Catharine A. MacKinnon, "Feminism, Marxism, Method, and the State," *Signs* 7 (1982), 515–44; *Signs* 8 (1983), 635–58; *Feminism Unmodified: Discourses on Life and Law* (Cambridge: Harvard University Press, 1987), esp. 172–83, 217–18; *Toward a Feminist Theory of the State* (Cambridge: Harvard University Press, 1989); "Reflections on Sex and Equality Under Law," *Yale Law Journal* 100 (1991), 1281–328.

11. MacKinnon, *Toward a Feminist Theory of the State,* 173. See also "Reflections on Sex and Equality," 1304: "The view that women seek out and enjoy forced sex is pure special pleading for the accused. This is the perspective the law has taken."

12. See, generally, Mary Belenky et al., *Women's Ways of Knowing* (New York: Basic Books, 1986).

many jurisdictions now acknowledge the reality of such silenced women by, for example, admitting evidence relating to battered woman syndrome—a condition of "learned helplessness"[13]—in cases where women claim to have killed or wounded a spouse or boyfriend in order to escape an abusive relationship.

The response to MacKinnon is developed in the literature by such legal theorists as Robin West and Ruth Colker.[14] West holds that to dismiss a priori as inauthentic pieces of false consciousness a woman's desire for sex is to assume either that the pleasure she seeks is not her own or that what she experiences is not experienced as pleasurable but merely reported as such. Yet, replies West, there are no non–theory-driven reasons to accept either assumption, as both fail to acknowledge the actual lived experiences of at least many women—their own subjective, phenomenological reports. Acknowledging women's actual voices, however, according to West, reveals that at least some women claim to derive pleasure from fantasies of domination and have a genuine desire for erotic submission. Colker insists that it is unclear what form the expression of a woman's "authentic" sexuality would take, and therefore no reason to discount any form of erotic expression, including heterosexually submissive relationships, as possibly authentic, as aspects of the woman's overall conception of the good. To the extent that West and Colker are right, aggressive, noncommunicative sex cannot, solely because it is noncommunicative, be discounted as unreasonable. The tension between the MacKinnon position and the West position, then, poses a double threat to Pineau's analysis. On the one hand, Pineau risks being pinned in a dilemma: either what women communicate is inauthentic and thus nonconsensual, or what they authentically communicate is (at least sometimes) a desire for noncommunicative sex. On the other hand, the mere fact of such large disagreements among feminist theorists reveals that the demand that the standard of reason-

13. *State v. Leidholm* 344 N.W.2d 811 (1983) at 819.

14. See Robin West, "The Difference in Women's Hedonic Lives: A Phenomenological Critique of Feminist Legal Theory," in Fineman and Thomadsen, eds., *At the Boundaries of Law* (New York: Routledge, 1991); Ruth Colker, "Feminism, Sexuality, and Authenticity," in ibid., 135–47. For a general review and discussion of this position, see Kathryn Abrams, "Ideology and Women's Choices," *Georgia Law Review* 24 (1990), 761–801.

ableness for consent or belief about consent reflect the "woman's point of view" is itself far from unproblematic.

The core of Pineau's critique of the traditional doctrinal understanding of consent is that it has been articulated and administered in a deeply gender-biased manner. The communicative criterion effects a much-needed shift from a hopelessly skewed standard to a workably impartial standard. It is an assumption of Pineau's argument that a communicative sexual act could not be such that it would be unreasonable for a woman to have acquiesced in it—not possible that the sex be nonconsensual—and yet also such that the defendant could have reasonably believed that it *was* consensual. This is to suppose that the dialectical starting points from which each person begins, the inferences each will take, the epistemic paths each will pursue ultimately, do converge in a way that will show each to be in like manner alive to the mutuality of desire. But if one takes seriously the fundamental feminist insight that the experiences one has and the way one conceptualizes them, that the beliefs one acquires, the inferential paths one takes through those beliefs, and the epistemic norms guiding one's selection can be influenced by one's gender-identity—can track gendered features of the world—then it is not impossible to see how the understandings of communicative lovers could come apart, and come apart in ways that raise serious questions about the fairness of holding persons to a stringent epistemic duty.

In *Rusk,* the defendant and the victim gave revealingly different accounts of what took place: she described one of his actions as "light choking," he described it as a "heavy caress." While the jury seems rightly to have doubted this defendant's sincerity, Estrich correctly observes that in similar cases of divergent descriptions it could turn out that both are accurate: what is unpleasant or frightening to one could sincerely be seen as erotic or pleasing to the other. The potential for disparities between such first-person reports seems best explained by the operation of socially constructed sex-role expectations, beliefs, and attitudes. And this raises a question of fairness for the communicative model: Can it be expressed and administered impartially where the parties may not be equally alive to the mutuality of desire?

The communicative model would appear to set up the following standard against which the trier of fact must judge the defendant's conduct: Did the defendant behave as the ordinary and prudent erotic conversationalist would have behaved under the circumstances? The judge or jury must then attempt to answer this question by seeking responses to a series of more specific questions: Did the defendant ask if she desired to be touched? Did the defendant ask if she wanted to be caressed? Did the defendant ascertain that she did desire intercourse? Yet these may, of course, be questions that were neither asked nor answered in so unambiguous a fashion. Persons on a date could, of course, most easily discharge their epistemic duty to ascertain mutuality by working through a checklist or by asking their partner to fill out a questionnaire. Naturally, this would destroy the very mutuality of desire which the couple seeks to create, less a genuine erotic conversation then a drab interrogation. It is because the requirement of being an erotic conversationalist calls into play a richer, more complex and subtle range of abilities than is displayed by the crude interrogator that the question of whether someone has satisfied that requirement can be contested.

Persons engaged in communicative sexuality, says Pineau, should instantiate the values of good conversationalists: they should be intuitive, sympathetic, and charitable. It is not unlikely, however, that the range and depth of one's sympathy and the clarity of one's intuition will turn out, as an empirical fact about our culture, to be significantly gendered features of one's personality. The range of men's sympathies may not be co-extensive, in many cases, with those of women; their degree of sensitivity and psychological insight, their understanding of subtle cues and signals—all of which are central to being a good conversationalist—may differ, in general, from those of women. A growing body of empirical data and sociolinguistic research supports this proposition. A recent, major study[15] documents both the pervasiveness of rape-supportive attitudes in contemporary American culture and the degree to which differences in such attitudes break down along sexual lines. The study specifically finds, for example, that men tend to give a uniformly more sexual reading to various behaviors and conversations than women do.[16] Another recent work by sociolinguist Deb-

---

15. The *Ms.* report, published in Robin Warshaw, *I Never Called It Rape* (New York: Harper & Row, 1988).

16. Ibid., 35–47, 85, 120. See also "Men, Women Interpret Sexual Cues Differ-

orah Tannen[17] explains such results on the general theory that men and women operate with differing and often competing "gender-lects," styles and patterns of communication.[18] Many such differences, according to Tannen, occur on the level of "meta-messages, . . . information about the relations among the people involved and their attitudes toward what they are saying or doing and the people they are saying and doing it to."[19] For example, men and women in our culture, Tannen argues, tend to function with different conceptions of what makes for important communication. Most women adopt an indirect conversational style as a way of establishing a sense of community or even intimacy with co-conversants; they tend to communicate in ways that foster rapport and facilitate negotiation. Men, on the whole, communicate in ways that will indicate their place within a social hierarchy, one that will emphasize their status and independence; for men, communication is largely a vehicle for displaying skill and knowledge, giving reports and detached descriptions of events. These stylistic differences, in turn, generate conflicts: men simply are not as communicative as women, and even silence is often understood differently by women and men;[20] unlike women, men frequently react to certain conversations as threats to their independence;[21] and women and men have different ways of signaling that they are listening to one another.[22]

---

ently," *Stanford Observer,* January–February 1991, 15, citing results of a study finding, inter alia, that when asked "whether such activities as going back to a date's room, kissing, French kissing, and taking off one's shirt indicate an interest in and willingness to have sex, men consistently interpreted all of those behaviors as more indicative of consent than women did."

17. Deborah Tannen, *You Just Don't Understand: Women and Men in Conversation* (New York: Ballantine Books, 1990).

18. Ibid., 42.

19. Ibid., 32.

20. See ibid., 81ff.

21. See ibid., 151. Tannen cites a study involving "a young man who, in discussing his sexual relationship with his girlfriend, told [researchers], 'We were in bed and she was saying, "Do this lighter," or "Do this softer," and I just told her that I was making love to her and she was going to have to let me do it my own way. . . . You don't want to feel bossed around.' "

22. Ibid., 142: "Not only do women give more listening signals . . . but the signals they give have different meanings for men and women, consistent with the speaker/audience alignment. Women use 'yeah' to mean 'I'm with you, I follow,' whereas men tend to say 'yeah' only when they agree. The opportunity for misunderstanding is

The foregoing results have obvious implications for the communicative model of reasonableness in rape law. Suppose, for example, that the defendant, under cross-examination, is asked whether the woman overtly communicated a desire to be touched. He responds by saying, "No, but the look in her eyes told me she wanted that." It is not readily apparent how critics of the traditional doctrinal approach to consent can entirely discount the genuinely communicative nature of such a response, assuming it is a sincere report. After all, it is precisely the law's failure to regard seriously what a woman takes to be communicated through the eyes of her assailant that critics like Estrich find so objectionable in the traditional doctrine.

The same point may be put another way. Onora O'Neill argues that the fundamental difficulty in ascertaining consent lies in the fact that consent, like other propositional attitudes, is referentially opaque: "When we consent to another's proposals we consent, even when 'fully' informed, only to some specific formulation of what the other has it in mind to do. We may remain ignorant of further, perhaps equally pertinent, accounts of what is proposed, including some to which we would not consent."[23] But this is to understate the difficulty. The problem is not simply that the miscommunications and cognitive misunderstandings which frequently plague erotic discourse arise because consent fails to be realized in a context transparent with respect to all of the various descriptions under which sexual activity can fall. The problem is not only that consent to an act under one description (for example, "petting") does not encompass whatever is entailed or conversationally implied by that description, for to state the problem in this way suggests that the parties are, *ab initio,* at least equally situated with regard to appreciating what those entailments and implications are. The deeper problem is, of course, that the assumptions behind and implications of consenting to an act de-

---

clear. When a man is confronted with a woman who has been saying 'yeah,' 'yeah,' 'yeah,' and then turns out not to agree, he may conclude that she has been insincere, or that she was agreeing without really listening. When a woman is confronted with a man who does *not* say 'yeah'—or much of anything else—she may conclude that *he* hasn't been listening. The men's style is more literally focused on the message level of talk, while the women's is focused on the relationship or metamessage level."

23. Onora O'Neill, "Between Consenting Adults," *Philosophy and Public Affairs* 14 (1985), 252–77.

scribed in one or another way are themselves gendered—that is, more readily available to, or overlooked by, members of one or the other gender.

All this said, of course, Rusk and defendants like him might be convictable under the communicative standard when they would not be convictable under traditional doctrine. Their conviction, moreover, would be a great virtue of the communicative criterion. Nonetheless, there will likely be some cases in which the law's expectations for erotic discourse may not be so readily satisfied. Of this we must remain mindful as we seek to achieve the reformist objectives demanded by a moral critique of existing rape law.

3

Date Rape and the Law: Another Feminist View

Catharine Pierce Wells

I want to begin my discussion by applauding Lois Pineau's clarity of vision and her strong defense of a woman's right to choose the nature of her own sexual relationships. The ideal of sexual self-expression for women is often obscured by the invocation of sexist stereotypes. As Pineau notes, there are recurring suggestions that women are manipulative in their sexual conduct and that they are caught in a conflict between powerful sexual desire and an equally powerful need to deny such desire.[1] In addition, society is inundated with images of female sexuality that are pornographic in the sense that they objectify and degrade women. Amid all this, Pineau's aspirations for women seem both authentic and refreshing. Thinking that women should be able to have sex in an uncoerced

---

1. Pineau, "Date Rape: A Feminist Analysis," reprinted as Chapter 1 of this book.

and unencumbered fashion is surely the right place to begin in sorting through the heated arguments over date rape.

Pineau's article aims at two related objectives. First, she attempts to redefine the legal elements of rape (or a somewhat lesser crime of sexual assault) from a feminist perspective. To do this, she must articulate a feminist conception of sexual consent. And this forms the basis of her second project, which is to reconceptualize sexual relationships on the basis of a communicative rather than a contractual model. Thus, she is working on a specific legal agenda and at the same time on a more general contribution to the ongoing discussion of nonsexist sexual practices. The thrust of my comments is that Pineau's article is unpersuasive in its legal analysis but interesting and provocative in its challenge to reconsider our sexual practices.

To summarize, I will make two lawyerly points and two more feminist objections to Pineau's work. The two lawyerly points are:

1. That Pineau is wrong in arguing that the criminal law should assess the reasonableness of the alleged rapist's conduct from the women's point of view.

2. That, while requiring women to show active resistance in order to show nonconsent is wrong, Pineau's proposal that the defendant show ongoing intimate communication goes much too far in the opposite direction.

The two feminist objections are:

3. That Pineau articulates an ideal of sexuality that is not necessarily shared by all women.

4. That she derives her vision of sexuality from an abstract and utopian perspective. Feminist theory, to the contrary, should be rooted in practice and attentive to the power imbalance that affects interactions between men and women.

Before proceeding, I'd like to say a little about the legal discussion that follows. Pineau is a philosopher and not a lawyer. Her discussion of the current state of rape law contains many errors and is probably too pessimistic in its inherent suggestion that nothing but the most egregious cases of rape can be prosecuted.[2] When we view her proposals as an agenda for legal reform, she should also be faulted for giving virtually no consideration to issues of fairness as they apply to the alleged rapist. Even though I agree with Pineau that the law of rape does not provide adequate redress for rape victims, I am also concerned that individual criminal defendants are not scapegoated for societal sexism. Criminal liability is a serious matter—it is hardly the place to experiment with rearrangements of social relations. Thus, the bottom line for me will be that, in most circumstances, women who accuse men of criminal date rape must have explicitly stated that sex was unwelcome.[3] I conclude this even though I recognize that there are many reasons why women remain silent when they are genuinely unwilling to have sex. But, while I believe that men are wrong to take advantage in such cases, I also believe that these are cases where criminal penalties are not appropriate.

1. *Whose perspective should determine whether the rapist has acted without the woman's consent?*

Pineau's legal case rests upon two central claims. First there is the claim that men and women differ in their understanding of rape. A woman may well be resisting what she perceives as coercion, while the man interprets her conduct as coyness or as an unwillingness to acknowledge her own sexual desire. Traditionally, alleged rapists have been able to defend themselves on the ground that they held a sincere belief that consent was present and that this belief was reasonable. Thus, the issue of reasonable belief is central in determining criminal liability, and Pineau's second claim is that the way to address this issue is to look at it from a woman's point of view rather than from a male perspective.

Pineau's arguments for this second claim are not persuasive. For example, she argues that courts are speaking from a male perspective when they speak as though nothing the woman does, short of shooting her assailant, will count as nonconsent. While it is true

2. For a comprehensive discussion of rape law from its common law beginnings to the feminist reforms of the 1970s, see Estrich, *Real Rape.*

3. I say "in most circumstances" because one can certainly think of hypothetical exceptions. For example, a "date" might physically prevent the victim from articulating her objections.

that this extreme version of the "male" perspective has been frequently invoked, it is also true that there are other, more suitable ways to deal with this extreme viewpoint. What is needed is not necessarily a female perspective, but rather some more objective way to determine the reasonableness of the assailant's belief.[4] The issue should not be whether there is some sexist story the defendant can tell to support his belief that the woman who says "NO!" really means yes. Rather the jury should consider whether a *reasonable* person in the defendant's position would have *reasonable* grounds for believing that consent had been given. In conforming to this standard of reasonableness, defendants are not entitled to cling to prejudice and self-serving ignorance. Reasonable people— male or female—are certainly capable of understanding that "NO!" means no.

Pineau also argues that we should utilize the woman's perspective because it is the woman's consent that is at the heart of the issue to be resolved. To the contrary, however, her consent is but a subsidiary question; the ultimate issue in the case is the culpability of the defendant—whether he engaged in conduct that warrants punishment in the criminal justice system. Since the basis of criminal liability is intentionally wrong or unreasonable conduct, fairness seems to require that we do not disregard his viewpoint entirely. For example, suppose that a woman grew up in a culture where touching someone on the breast was a common form of greeting. Thus, when the defendant touched her there, she smiled pleasantly and invitingly. If the defendant does not know this fact about her culture and sincerely believes that she has given her consent to further intimacies, should his judgment of consent be viewed as unreasonable merely because, from her perspective, she had done no more than say hello? It does not seem fair to resolve this issue solely by examining her perspective. Nor, as noted above, does a standard that requires reasonable belief permit the defendant to rely on prejudice and ignorance. The proper inquiry here is not just what the defendant knew but also what he reason-

---

4. It is traditional for legal theorists to make a distinction between a "subjective" standard that measures the actual beliefs of legal actors and an "objective" standard that compares actual beliefs with what is reasonable under the circumstances. But see Dolores A. Donovan and Stephanie M. Wildman, "Is the Reasonable Man Obsolete? A Critical Perspective on Self-Defense and Provocation," *Loyola of Los Angeles Law Review* 14 (1981), 435–68.

ably could have been expected to know or to find out. And it is this inquiry that is central to determining guilt in a rape case; we do not simply ask what the women's perspective says, but rather should consider how much of the women's perspective this defendant had an obligation to discover.

2. *Pineau's proposal that the defendant be required to prove consent by showing ongoing intimate communication is too extreme.*

There should be no question that when a woman says "NO!" she means no. On the other hand, Pineau's proposed standard in rape cases would permit a conviction even if the woman is merely silent or if her responses are not enthusiastic and encouraging. In going so far, it condemns many forms of sexual intercourse that we ought to be reluctant to classify as criminal. Let me give some examples.

The first example is a typical scene from a romance novel. The handsome hero sweeps a charming but inexperienced woman off her feet. She does not object, nor does she offer much encouragement. For her, the romance of the situation is enhanced by the fact that she feels overwhelmed by the hero's strong (single-minded) and silent (noncommunicative) pursuit of sexual pleasure. Certainly, the woman who "succumbs" in such circumstances does not have a self-empowering view of her own sexuality. And perhaps there are many women who would find the hero neither sexy nor ethical. However, if millions of women buy such novels and describe these scenes as "sexy," can we really convict a man of rape when he interprets his partner's conduct in the context of this story? Is it so unreasonable for a man in this society to construe such silence as consent? Under such circumstances, shouldn't we at least require that the woman say "NO!"?

A second example involves the case of a sweet but not very sophisticated young man who has sex with a seemingly willing partner. He is later arrested for rape and takes the stand in his own defense. He testifies that the woman voiced no objections and that their sexual intimacies had progressed in a state of total silence. Despite the silence, he nevertheless believed that she was a willing participant. Under a standard of reasonable belief, this man would probably be acquitted if the jury believes his testimony. Under Pineau's standard, however, he could be convicted because the sexual encounter is noncommunicative. Certainly, there are many explanations for the lack of communication. Perhaps the young man (and maybe even the young woman herself) are not very articulate. Perhaps they are embarrassed to speak concretely about the mechanics of sexual pleasure. Perhaps they are simply uninterested (for whatever reason) in communicating with each other. We might well wish that things were different for these young people, but convicting the man of rape seems like an excessive way to express our disapproval.

Finally, it would seem that Pineau's proposed definition of sexual assault creates a possibility that women could be convicted of the crime. Suppose that a woman wants to have sexual intercourse with her date and aggressively pursues that outcome. He is reluctant, and if asked in unpressured circumstances would state a preference to abstain. He does not, however, at any point in the evening say (or even hint) that her sexual attention is unwelcome. Nevertheless, his description of his own behavior, if believed, would lead a detached observer to think that he had not been very enthusiastic. Can the woman be convicted of rape? Under the standard consent theory, she cannot. Under Pineau's legal requirement of communicative sex, why not?

3. *Pineau's communicative ideal of sexuality is not necessarily shared by all women.*

Feminist method involves a reexamination of legal and moral questions from a "woman's perspective." This, in turn, requires that we be able to describe something called "women's experience." I have used quotation marks in order to suggest that phrases like "woman's perspective" and "women's experience" need more careful attention. The difficulty with these concepts is that not all women have the same experiences or share the same perspective. Nevertheless, there are many cases where the nature of the "woman's perspective" seems obvious—at least by contrast with a more dominant "male perspective." Thus, when arguments about consent are based on claims that a woman didn't fight hard enough, and when these arguments are readily accepted by male judges and jurors, then surely feminists are correct in seeing a "male perspective" at work. The "woman's perspective," by contrast, acknowledges that it is difficult for rape victims to resist vigorously when they are likely to be overwhelmed by terror. In such cases, feminist analysis plays an important role by reminding us of the inherent bias in the male perspective. But if we leave such extremes or try to reconstruct a positive ideal of how sexual conduct should go, the concepts of "women's experience" or a "woman's perspective" seem much less salient.

More and more feminists are recognizing that arguments that begin with some universal characterization of female experience suffer from the problem of essentialism.[5] To criticize an analysis as essentialist is to recognize that all women do not share the same experience. In part, this is because the experience of gender intersects with other societal hierarchies such as race, class, and sexual preference. Thus, the writings of academic feminists sometimes suffer from the same bias or partiality of perspective that limits the "male viewpoint." When white, heterosexual academic women describe "women's experience," they often simply project their own experience to all women. The resulting picture is "women's experience" as experienced by white, heterosexual, educated, articulate, upper-middle-class, and relatively independent women. Using such projections to remake the world from a "feminist" perspective may well marginalize the interests and experience of large numbers of women who do not share these characteristics. For this reason, it is important to think carefully about the sort of experiential claims that underlie Pineau's article.

The ideal of sexuality that Pineau articulates is based on the Kantian idea that it is wrong for a person to treat another person as a mere means to an end. In a sexual context, Pineau argues that this requires a communicative form of sexual relationship that results in a mutuality of sexual pleasure. Her vision is "feminist" in the sense that it rejects certain "male" models of sexual expression. For example, the ideal of communicative sex provides a basis for criticizing the kind of objectified sex that is found in pornography. Further, in honoring individuality and choice, it seems to avoid at least the most obvious forms of heterosexism. Any form

5. See, e.g., Elizabeth V. Spelman, *Inessential Woman* (Boston: Beacon Press, 1988); Angela Harris, "Race and Essentialism in Feminist Legal Theory," *Stanford Law Review* 42 (1990), 581; and Pat Cain, "Feminist Jurisprudence: Grounding the Theories," *Berkeley Women's Law Journal* 4 (1989), 191–214.

of sexual practice will be all right so long as it is not exploitive or inexpressive. Thus, in these terms at least, Pineau's vision seems to have a "feminist" tone. Nevertheless, as we think more deeply about the concrete reality of women's lives, we might wonder whether Pineau's conception is truly the product of a "woman's perspective." What do women—actual women, not theoretical (or Kantian) women—want from their sexual experience? When we ask the question this way, it is obvious that women's sexual interests cannot be defined in any one construct. There are, in fact, many women who share a "masterful seduction" view of sex and romance. There are women who support themselves by prostitution or by marriage to wealthy men. There are lesbians who enjoy patterns of domination and subordination that are commonly found in "male" pornography. In short, millions of women do not seek—and may not want—the kind of communicative sexual relationships that Pineau describes. What should feminists say to them—that they are wrong? that they are falsely conscious? that they have fallen short of Kantian ideals?

4. *Pineau's theory is not rooted in practice and is inattentive to the power relations that affect interactions between men and women.*

Feminists have criticized traditional forms of theory-building for tolerating a large gulf between theory and practice. Feminist theory cannot tolerate such a gulf because it aims at the real world transformation of women's lives. Thus, feminist theory begins with the here and now of a sexist society and seeks to analyze these realities in a way that is helpful and empowering to women.

Against this background, Pineau's analysis seems unduly utopian in its disconnection from the societal barriers that constrain women's choices. Catharine MacKinnon has argued that the widespread violence against women and their comparative poverty mean that sexual relations between men and women can never be truly consensual.[6] In addition, she suggests that even our most intimate feelings of sexual desire have been largely constructed and socialized by patriarchal power.[7] If MacKinnon is right, then Pineau's goal of simply freeing women to articulate their own de-

6. See, e.g., MacKinnon, *Toward a Feminist Theory of the State,* 127ff.
7. Ibid., 110.

sires cannot be a truly liberating alternative. In short, Pineau's analysis is flawed by the fact that she proceeds as though women were free to redefine their sexuality on an entirely blank slate.

I do not mean to suggest that there is nothing of value in a utopian project. Without question, society has suffered from a scarcity of strong women role-models. From fairy tales to prime-time television, strong women centered on their own needs are seen as ruthless and corrupt, while by contrast "good" women are portrayed as endlessly sensitive to the needs of others. And, without doubt, this conception of the "good" woman has something to do with the rape mythology Pineau describes. The "good" woman, to be sure, is careful not to arouse sexual needs that she is unwilling or unable to satisfy. Contesting this version of the "good" woman as it pertains to sex is an important project, and Pineau's description of communicative sexuality does just that by promoting the idea that both men and women would be better off if they took more responsibility for their own sexual desires and conduct. In a culture where women are socialized to respond to the needs and expectations of others, Pineau's vision reminds us that a different focus is possible.

Utopian projects can help us to internalize visions of women's lives that are not constrained by current expectations. They are useful so long as we remember that they describe a sense of potentiality and promise rather than marching orders in the feminist struggle. Fifteen years ago, for example, many writers popularized the notion that women could "have it all." Women should not settle for a career or a family, they urged. It was possible, they argued, to do both. Thus, many women aspired to become both supermom and fast-track careerist. Unfortunately, these competing aspirations ended up by subjecting women to endless rounds of self-recrimination as they began to understand that they were not able to do "it all" and be happy at the same time. Utopian ideals are a double-edged sword. They can provide hope and inspiration for self-empowerment, but when they are transplanted into the context of "good" womenhood, they may become just one more set of oppressive expectations.

The potential for oppression seems especially pertinent when we are talking about sexuality. Pineau complains that the media are too reluctant to deal with questions of sexual relations and sexual intimacy.[8] But to the contrary, it seems to me that sex is a major topic of media discussion. We should notice, however, that sex on television and in the movies is always the same: two attractive people melt without effort into a warm display of human passion. There is seldom any awkwardness or cause for complaint. Indeed, sex is sometimes even portrayed as the sensitive, communicative process that Pineau endorses. But popular culture—for all its sexual explicitness—does not reflect reality. There is little recognition of how much objectified, instrumental, indifferent, coerced, and passive sex is out there in the world. "Bad" sex is hard to talk about. It causes sadness and frustration. In a world where women are expected to slug it out in the marketplace without losing their femininity, "bad" sex for women entails both self-pity and self-reproach.

Thus, I end by stating my concerns about Pineau's requirement of communicative sexuality. In a world where many women (and some men) are powerless to communicate, it clearly harms the powerless to suggest that communication is morally required. Specifically, I worry that the relentless focus on ideal sex will impede the kind of candid discussion that enables women to raise their own consciousness and to reduce their exploitation. In short, my concern is that, given a world where women have little power over their own sexuality and a world where nonideal sex seems to be a topic unfit for discussion, the cost of limiting feminist analysis to utopian solutions may well be too high.

8. See Pineau, "Date Rape," 243.

4

Forcible Rape, Date Rape, and Communicative Sexuality: A Legal Perspective

Angela P. Harris

Introduction

Lois Pineau argues that "date rape" (defined as "nonconsensual sex that does not involve physical injury, or the explicit threat of physical injury")[1] does not look like a crime in this society because we think of male sexuality as naturally aggressive and uncontrollable, female sexuality as naturally submissive and controllable, and sexual pleasure as emergent from intercourse without the need for communication. Pineau shows this "aggressive-acquiescence" model of human sexuality to be internally incoherent and proposes a new model, "communicative sexuality," to replace it. In this vision of sexuality, both sexes are equally able to control their sexual impulses. More important, sexual pleasure does not emerge "naturally," but rather is the result of a kind of conversation in

---

1. Pineau, "Date Rape: A Feminist Analysis," 217. This article is reprinted as Chapter 1 of this book.

which each partner lets the other one know what is pleasurable and what is not.

For Pineau, communicative sexuality is not just a good idea; it ought to be the law. She takes the position that date rape should be a crime (though not as serious a crime as "forcible rape") and that it will properly be treated as such if the law of rape takes communicative sexuality rather than aggressive acquiescence as the touchstone of reasonable sexual behavior.[2] In this chapter, I comment on her argument from a legal perspective. I argue that although at least one jurisdiction, California, has recently moved toward both establishing communicative sexuality as an underlying model of sexual behavior and criminalizing date rape, Pineau's recommendation that communicative sexuality be taken not simply as a behavioral ideal but as a legal standard in rape cases is nevertheless problematic for at least two reasons.

First, Pineau's assumption that changing the substantive law of rape will change the outcome of date rape cases is too simple. Toward the end of the article, Pineau writes: "All that is needed . . . in order to provide women with legal protection from 'date rape' is to make both reckless indifference and willful ignorance a sufficient condition of *mens rea* and to make communicative sexuality the accepted norm of sex to which a reasonable woman would agree." I argue that even if these conditions were met (and one of them has obtained in California since 1872), the law on the books must still be interpreted by judges, juries, and attorneys. For date rape to be taken truly seriously as a crime, communicative sexuality must be a social as well as a legal norm.

This dilemma leads to another. Pineau's article seems to take the position that the presence or absence of consent should be determined from a "woman's point of view."[3] But if the reasonable woman's perspective on when sex becomes rape really is different from the reasonable man's point of view, then a serious problem arises from a legal perspective. For the law of rape has two competing goals: not only to protect women from nonconsensual intercourse but also to "ensur[e] that men are not convicted of felonies

2. For a similar argument from a legal perspective, see "Shifting the Communication Burden: A Meaningful Consent Standard in Rape," *Harvard Women's Law Journal* 6 (1983), 143.
3. Pineau, "Date Rape," 221.

they could not reasonably have known they were committing."[4]
To the extent that Pineau is suggesting that communicative sexuality is sexuality "from a woman's perspective," rather than simply a human perspective, the fairness of its incorporation into the criminal law becomes questionable.

A Short History of California Rape Law

The 1872 Law of Rape: Aggression and Acquiescence

In 1872, the year the California Legislature first organized its statutes into codes, section 261 of the California Penal Code defined rape as "an act of sexual intercourse accomplished with a female, not the wife of the perpetrator" which occurred under a number of listed circumstances. These circumstances fell into three distinct categories. First, it was rape if the woman was incapable of giving consent. This could be so because of her age (in 1872, girls under the age of ten were legally incapable of giving consent), or by reason of her mental status—for instance, if she were insane, or if she were unconscious and the defendant was aware of that fact. Second, heterosexual intercourse outside of marriage was rape when the defendant had committed a fraud which persuaded the woman that the defendant was her husband. The third category of rape is the important one for our purposes—the one which has come to be called "forcible rape." In 1872, forcible rape occurred "where [the woman] resists, but her resistance is overcome by force or violence," and also "[w]here she is prevented from resisting by threats of immediate and great bodily harm, accompanied by apparent power of execution."[5]

California's 1872 definition of rape clearly reflects Pineau's aggressive-acquiescence model of sexuality. Sexual intercourse only becomes rape under the most extreme circumstances—when the

---

4. Ibid., 146. I shall speak of a male defendant and a female victim throughout this chapter, although many modern rape statutes are sex-neutral. See, e.g., Cal. Penal C. §261 (West 1991).

5. California, therefore, never followed the strictest definition of forcible rape, which required the victim to physically resist "to the utmost." See Estrich, "Rape," *Yale Law Journal* 95 (1986), 1122.

female is nine years old or younger, when she is insane, when the man has wrongfully persuaded her they are married, or when he knows she is unconscious (her sexuality is so passive and his so aggressive that she may slip into a swoon without his noticing it). (The annotators muse: "Whether it is to be regarded as possible that a connection should be accomplished during the unconsciousness of natural sleep, without arousing the female, is said to be an open question in medical jurisprudence.")[6] Even when the rape is committed by means of threatening force, only the most extreme circumstances negate consent: the threats must be of *immediate* and *great* bodily harm (threats of retaliation, threats to her children, or threats of minor bodily harm apparently being too consistent with seduction). As Pineau notes, such a legal regime makes sense if women are expected to be coy about their sexuality—if they must be simultaneously sexual desirers and sexual deniers. Proof of vigorous resistance by the woman is necessary to demonstrate her sincerity.

The 1991 Law of Rape: Toward Communicative Sexuality

Much has happened to section 261 of the California Penal Code since 1872, and in 1991 California moved significantly closer to Pineau's vision of a world in which aggressive-acquiescent sex is presumptively unreasonable and date rape is clearly a crime. The 1991 version of section 261 no longer defines rape as a sex-specific crime, but as "an act of sexual intercourse accomplished with a person not the spouse of the perpetrator," under a list of particular circumstances.[7] Although in 1991 the circumstances which make sexual intercourse into rape fall into the same three categories of incapacity, fraud, and coercion that the law recognized in 1872, the forcible rape definition has changed significantly. The description of what constitutes a valid threat to turn sex into rape has expanded considerably. For example, not only threats of retaliation but threats to use the authority of a public official against the victim or another are now sufficient.

6. Note to Cal. Penal C. §261 at 113 (Haymond & Burch, annot. 1872).

7. Moreover, although the definition of rape in section 261 still fails to recognize nonconsensual sex between spouses as a crime, section 262, added to the Penal Code in 1979, recognizes the crime of spousal rape. Spousal rape, however, continues to be a less serious crime than rape by someone other than one's spouse.

More important, the requirement that a woman physically resist her attacker had disappeared from the statute by 1991. In its place, the statute provides that it is rape if sexual intercourse occurs "where it is accomplished against a person's will by means of force, violence, duress, menace, or fear of immediate and unlawful bodily injury on the person of another." Of particular interest here are the words "duress" and "menace," which were added to the statute in 1990. The original draft of the 1990 amendment would simply have deleted everything after "will," so that sexual intercourse would constitute rape where it was accomplished against a person's will,[8] and perhaps this change would have best accomplished Pineau's aim. But this approach was rejected in the second draft of the bill, and duress and menace were instead added to the preexisting categories of force, violence, and fear of immediate bodily harm.

"Duress" is defined in the 1991 version of section 261 as follows:

> [A] direct or implied threat of force, violence, danger, hardship, or retribution sufficient to coerce a reasonable person of ordinary susceptibilities to perform an act which otherwise would not have been performed, or acquiesce in an act to which one otherwise would not have submitted. The total circumstances, including the age of the victim, and his or her relationship to the defendant, are factors to consider in appraising the existence of duress.[9]

"Menace" is defined as "any threat, declaration, or act which shows an intention to inflict an injury upon another."[10]

In 1991, Pineau's story of the woman who feels paradoxically at the end of the evening both that she has been raped and that she has let herself be raped becomes a story that the law is willing to take seriously. Her date has not shown menace, but surely she has been under duress: his "aggressive body contact," his "hostile stance," as well as her own uncertainty, have caused her to acquiesce in an act in which she otherwise would not have participated.

8. SB 2586 (Roberti).
9. Cal. Penal C. §261(b) (West 1991).
10. Cal. Penal C. §261(c) (West 1991).

But suppose her date, now a defendant in a rape case, argues that her acquiescence should be read as consent—that her decision to "go along and get it over with" under his blandishments turned rape back into sex? As of 1991 the California Penal Code included section 261.6, which reads as follows:

> In prosecutions under [various statutes, including §261], in which consent is at issue, "consent" shall be defined to mean positive cooperation in act or attitude pursuant to an exercise of free will. The person must act freely and voluntarily and have knowledge of the nature of the act or transaction involved.

Moreover, in 1990 the following language was added: "A current or previous dating relationship shall not be sufficient to constitute consent where consent is at issue in a prosecution under [section 261]."[11] If communicative sexuality is not yet the touchstone of reasonableness, Pineau's goal is nevertheless well within reach.

Law on the Books and Law in Action

If Pineau's analysis is right, this should be the happy ending to the story. Unfortunately, efforts at rape law reform have shown that statutory change alone is not enough to bring about changes in law enforcement.[12] Pineau's article anticipates a world in which the proper legislation, followed by a public information campaign, will effectively criminalize date rape. But the California experience shows that, rather than being a linear process, significant law reform can be frustratingly circular. In order for the reform to be effective, the judges, juries, and attorneys who interpret the new legal rule must already have absorbed the new norm; yet the source of the norm (at least in Pineau's model) is the rule itself. As a result, even the most sweeping legal changes can be vitiated by

---

11. Cal. Penal C. §261.6 (West 1991).

12. See, e.g., Marsh et al., *Rape and the Limits of Law Reform*, ix, arguing that Michigan's experience with rape reform indicates that "the reform brought about changes in procedure but not in basic attitudes or definitions of the crime."

judges, juries, and attorneys who have not yet internalized the new norm.

The California experience with the reasonable mistake of fact defense provides an example. Pineau argues: "All that is needed . . . to provide women with legal protection from 'date rape' is to make both reckless indifference and willful ignorance a sufficient condition of *mens rea* and to make communicative sexuality the accepted norm of sex to which a reasonable woman would agree." In terms of the law on the books, California's law in 1991 comes quite close to meeting both conditions. Since 1979, as we have seen, consent has been defined as positive cooperation through free, voluntary, and informed action, rather than mere acquiescence. Moreover, even in 1872 both willful ignorance of a woman's lack of consent and reckless indifference to her consent were sufficient mental states for criminal responsibility. This is so because in order for the defendant's "mistake" about the woman's consent to be a valid excuse, the mistake must be reasonable, not just sincere. Even a negligent defendant, then—a man who is not indifferent or willfully ignorant of his partner's nonconsent, but simply unreasonably careless in ascertaining her state of mind—may be guilty of rape under California law.

Yet despite these superficial movements toward a model of communicative sexuality, the ghost of the aggressive-acquiescence model lingers. In 1991 a California appellate court ruled that the jury must receive an instruction about the mistake defense whenever there is any evidence to support the defendant's claim, "no matter how weak or unconvincing that evidence may be," and no matter how far the defendant's story diverges from the victim's story—even in a case where the defense was *actual* consent rather than a good faith, though mistaken, *belief* in consent.[13] And evidence that the rape occurred on a date is still being used as sufficient to support giving an instruction on the defendant's reasonable mistake.[14] Perhaps these cases only illustrate that commu-

13. *People v. Williams*, 283 Cal.Rptr. 518, 522 (Cal.App. 1991). In a strongly worded dissent, Presiding Justice Low charged: "The majority decision reverts to that discredited mind-set which automatically views the woman's testimony regarding sexual assault with skepticism" (523).

14. *People v. May*, 213 Cal.App.3d 118, 261 Cal.Rptr. 502 (Cal.App. 1989). The court described the victim's initial encounter with the defendant as a "pick-up" and pointed to the fact that the victim had admitted some attraction to the defendant as

nicative sexuality has not yet become the legal standard of reasonableness, but I think they also show how difficult changing notions of reasonableness can be.

Any standard for what is "reasonable," after all, must appeal to the way things already are. It would surely be an admirable thing, for example, for all people to treat one another as brothers and sisters, but not reasonable to expect such global family-feeling. Installing communicative sexuality as the norm of reasonable sexual behavior entails more than creating and publicizing a legal rule; it also entails a change in social life such that judges, juries, and attorneys for both the defense and the prosecution can reconcile that norm with everyday experience. In legal language, the problem is that what is "reasonable" is not a pure question of law but a so-called "mixed question of law and fact"—an issue rooted in everyday experience, not just legal expertise.

Recently, legal attempts have been made to change what a jury considers "reasonable."[15] In several jurisdictions, for example, a battered woman on trial for assaulting or killing her batterer may now introduce expert testimony to dispel the jury's "reasonable" misapprehensions about battered women.[16] But altering attitudes about what consensual sexual behavior is "reasonable" will be a far more difficult task. It is one thing to change one's perspective

---

support for a mistake defense. The author of the opinion commented: "Maria's behavior in willingly accompanying him to the apartment after several hours of merriment, her failure to escape when presented with the opportunity, and her lack of verbal objection while in the bedroom could reasonably have been misinterpreted by May as the conduct of someone playing games rather than resisting his advances" (213 Cal.App.3d at 126).

It should be noted that this case was decided before the legislature added "duress" to the conditions that make sexual intercourse into rape and provided that a current or previous dating relationship shall not be sufficient to constitute consent. But the legislature's definition of consent as positive cooperation rather than acquiescence had been in force for ten years.

15. For a social-scientific analysis of various recent attempts to alter juries' views on what behavior is reasonable by way of expert testimony, see Vidmar and Schuller, "Juries and Expert Evidence: Social Framework Testimony," *Law and Contemporary Problems* 52 (1989), 133.

16. See, e.g., *State v. Kelly,* 97 N.J. 178, 478 A.2d 364 (1984). Evidence of "battered woman syndrome" has been slow to be accepted in California courts, however. See, e.g., *People v. Aris,* 215 Cal.App.3d 1200, 264 Cal.Rptr. 167 (Cal.App. 1989), upholding the trial court's exclusion of expert testimony that the defendant was a battered woman and how that affected her mental condition at the time she killed her husband.

on a defendant whose life experience may seem quite foreign, and another to adopt a mind-set that affects one's own experience with the world. More important, judgments of reasonableness are meant to reflect the judgments of the community, and not the judgments of a scientific or cultural elite. The very notion of imposing new standards for reasonable behavior from the top down, then, is in tension with traditional understandings of the roles of judge and jury.

The problem is even more intractable as a practical matter with respect to police and prosecutors, because their judgments are subject to far less meaningful review than the judgments of courts and juries. Until police officers and prosecutors have internalized a norm of communicative sexuality, then, decisions on who is arrested for rape and who is prosecuted will continue to be guided by the aggression-acquiescence model, despite statutory language to the contrary. A simple public education campaign about the law will not be enough to budge a person's knowledge about the way life is, yet without a change in social norms date rape will continue to be treated as noncriminal. Pineau's proposal, far from being a straightforward matter of political mobilization, opens up a dilemma in legal and social reform.

Whose Reasonableness?

But perhaps things are not as difficult as they seem, because at least some members of the community—that is, women—already understand communicative sexuality as the touchstone for reasonableness. At some points in her article, Pineau seems to take the position that in recognizing communicative sexuality as the norm the law would simply be recognizing women's point of view. For instance, she says: "What is often missing is the voice of the woman herself, an account of what it would be reasonable for *her* to agree to, that is to say, an account of what is reasonable from *her* standpoint." The task of social change will be far less onerous if half the population already recognizes communicative sexuality as the proper norm of sexual functioning.

In the civil context, the law has occasionally been known to recognize the "reasonable woman" standard as the proper gauge of conduct. For example, in a 1991 Ninth Circuit case, *Ellison v. Brady*,[17] the court held that in the context of Title VII, which makes sexual harassment an actionable civil claim, what constituted sexual harassment should be judged from the perspective of a "reasonable woman"—not a "reasonable man," as has been traditional in the law. The court adopted this standard over a "reasonable person" standard, on the theory that "a sex-blind reasonable person standard tends to be male-biased and tends to systematically ignore the experiences of women."[18] Similarly, one could argue, the line between consensual sexual intercourse and rape should be judged from the perspective of a reasonable woman, not a reasonable man or even a reasonable person.

But this approach does not solve the problem of reasonable mistake of fact. Even if actual consent is measured from the perspective of what a reasonable woman would feel, it must be a defense that a man might have reasonably, though wrongly, misconstrued her behavior. The reasonable mistake defense is not simply a concession to legal sexism; it reflects a recognition that the criminal law must respect the principle of *mens rea* in the broad sense, the so-called "culpability principle." Except for commercial regulatory offenses and offenses carrying very little penalty, such as traffic offenses, people are generally not punished in Anglo-American criminal law unless they are worthy of some measure of blame.[19]

Thus, unless a date rape conviction is to be treated as the equivalent of a traffic ticket—as perhaps it should?—we must be able to say with confidence that the defendant violated not just his victim's standard of conduct but his own as well.[20] The consequences of a criminal charge are far more severe than a civil suit, and it

17. 924 F.2d 872 (9th Cir. 1991).
18. 924 F.2d at 879.
19. Compare Sanford H. Kadish, "Criminal Sanctions for Economic Regulations," in *Blame and Punishment: Essays in the Criminal Law* (New York: Macmillan, 1987), 57, discussing "the use of the criminal sanction to prohibit and condemn behavior that threatens secular interests, but that is not regarded as fundamentally and inherently wrong."
20. See Estrich, "Rape," 1146: "[L]iability turns on the jury's judgment both of the woman's response and of the man's assessment (through the *mens rea* requirement) of the woman's response." Estrich argues that this "fair warning problem" is the result of the law's refusal either to create bright-line rules about when rape becomes sex regardless of the woman's behavior or to take the woman's statements of nonconsent as binding.

will not do to put a person in jail or prison for actions that did not to him seem unreasonable. Once again, then, we are up against the need for a society-wide change in norms and not simply a change in legal rules.

Pineau's analysis of the social myths underlying current rape law is insightful, and her proposal is a different vision of sexuality, provocative and persuasive. But her practical recommendations are more difficult and complex than they appear at first glance. Recognizing communicative sexuality rather than aggressive-acquiescence as the norm for human sexuality would make for a far happier society than the one we live in today, but law alone neither provides the solution nor the problem.

5

A Response to My Critics

Lois Pineau

Recent Developments in Law and Policy on Sexual Assault

I'll begin with a quick look at some legal and policy developments that have occurred since "Date Rape" was published. These developments are interesting in a number of respects. In the case of what has happened in Canada, they show, I believe, the ultimate practicality of the approach that I recommend. In Canada, communicative standards for consent to sexual activity have received the concrete wording, and the judicial interpretation of that wording, required to bring the law into line with what is reasonable from what I have called a "woman's point of view." At Antioch College a similar attempt to develop a policy on sexual assault and consent based on the communicative model has been made, using language that is more specific than the legalese of the Canadian Criminal Code. In California, however, recent changes to the Penal Code fall short of what is needed. It is instructive to look at why further

revisions are desirable. The purpose of reviewing these three policies is to provide a background against which the skepticism expressed, even by those who support adoption of a communicative
model of sexuality, can be assessed.

Canadian Law

Recent amendments to the Criminal Code of Canada have enabled
the Canadian courts to move toward a standard of communicative
sexuality which goes beyond what I even dreamed possible at the
time that I wrote my article "Date Rape."

The crucial section of the Criminal Code now states that among
other things there is no consent if "the complainant expresses, by
words or conduct, a lack of agreement to engage in the activity;
or the complainant having consented to engage in sexual activity,
expresses, by words or conduct, a lack of agreement to continue to
engage in the activity" (§273.1(2)(d)(e)).

Section 273.2(b) states: "It is not a defence for the accused to say
that he believed the complainant consented, if the accused did not
take reasonable steps, in the circumstances known to the accused
at the time, to ascertain that the complainant was consenting."
Section 273.1(e) states: there is no consent where "the complainant, having consented to engage in sexual activity, expresses, by
words or conduct, a lack of agreement to continue to engage in the
activity."

Two things are crucial to applying these clauses. The first is that
words and conduct be given their normal meaning. The second is
that "taking reasonable steps" be given enough content that it no
longer becomes reasonable to proceed with sexual activity despite
a woman's resistance and stated objections.

Fortunately, the judiciary's interpretation of both these clauses
has been progressive. The courts require that "positive steps" be
taken in order to satisfy the condition that "reasonable steps be
taken" to determine whether a complainant is really consenting.
Clause 273.1(e) has been interpreted to mean that consent must be
obtained on a step-by-step basis.

Taken together with other sections of the code, the above clauses
provide unprecedented protection against sexual assault: (1) the
requirement of taking reasonable steps makes the defense of honest belief more difficult. Unless reasonable efforts were made by

the accused to determine whether the complainant really consented, no defense of honest belief is likely to succeed. (2) Any sexual liberties taken with respect to the body without consent constitute sexual assault. (3) Evidence that the accused believed the complainant consented must be independent of his testimony and have an "air of reality" which may be conferred by all the circumstances in which the alleged assault took place. (4) If there is no "air of reality" to the defense of honest belief, the jury may not consider it.

A recent case illustrates the practical implications of the revised law. The case involves a high school boy's conviction for sexual assault. The boy had been engaged in kissing and caressing his date, an activity to which she had consented. The boy, without her consent, stuck his hand under the woman's shirt, and touched her breast. The woman pushed his hand away, and the encounter came to an end, but her parents reported the incident to the police, who charged the boy.

In assuming the right to touch the breast without permission, the court held, the boy assaulted her.[1] The judge was very clear. Consent to the kisses was not to be taken as consent to the touching of the breast. The decision assumed that consent to one kind of sexual act cannot be taken as consent to another kind. And the boy was guilty because he failed to take reasonable steps to determine whether it was all right to touch the woman's breast.

The Antioch Policy

At Antioch College in Ohio, a campus policy on sexual assault was developed through an intensive consultative process with students, administrators, and faculty. The process resulted in a criterion for sexual assault that is even narrower in its requirements than the legalese of the Canadian Criminal Code. The short rule is that persons who wish to engage in sexual activity must ask explicitly, and that negative answers must be given their normal meaning. The policy requires as well that each new kind of sexual activ-

---

1. *R. v. W.* (p.) (December 8, 1993) Doc. CA C10992, C11203, C11319, C11457, C11458, C11459 (Ont. C.A.) Affirming (Feb. 20, 1992) Lock, HJ (Ont. General Division).

ity must be explicitly consented to. According to this policy, only clear verbal expression will suffice to convey consent.

According to the Antioch code, the dialogue during sexual activity could be expected to include the following sorts of questions: "Can I kiss you?" "Can I touch your breast?" "Would you like me to touch you everywhere?" "Do you want to fuck?" Alternatively, it could include blanket questions asked right at the beginning: "Do you want to sleep with me?"

Is this going overboard? Do we really have to require positive questions ahead of time? Why shouldn't merely negative gestures suffice: he touched her breast and she pushed him away?

The feeling that these requirements are too stringent, that they fail to accord with too much that is normal activity, comes from our understanding of the behavior of professed lovers. When I meet my lover, I kiss him without asking. Sometimes I come up behind him and put my arms around him. But I am in no doubt whatever that he is my lover. We have talked about it. We have exchanged promises. There have been no intervening occasions which have called our relationship into question.

Professions of love and loyalty which have been accepted, and which there is no reason to think have been put on hold, would seem to stand proxy as having taken reasonable steps to determine the acceptability of kisses and hugs, and even of more intimate caresses, ahead of time. Admitting this, however, may seem to border on dangerous territory. We do not want to find ourselves in the position of agreeing that having accepted a lover once commits one to accepting him for all time, or that marriage is a carte blanche for rape. However, I do not think this is a problem so long as "no" still means no, and any negative responses, even among lovers, are seen as "withdrawing consent with respect to continuing the love act."

The Antioch policy is designed to provide guidelines primarily for dating students on campus, many of whom will not know each other all that well and many of whom will not be professed lovers who have exchanged promises. This is typical of a campus context, and there are many good reasons for adopting the Antioch policy in that context. The first is that it is harmless. If you're going to have sex, it doesn't hurt anyone or anything if you own up to what you are doing. The second is that it may very well enhance the eroticism of sexual activity to talk about it as well as to engage in it. The third is that the policy induces everyone, both men and women, to take responsibility for their erotic desires. The fourth is that the openness of this approach protects both men and women from being victimized by those who, where there is a lack of clear words, may act on interpretations that are ill-grounded and self-serving. The only proviso I would add, therefore, is that lovers who have previously acknowledged themselves as lovers, who have made a mutual promise to be lovers, be excluded from the step-by-step approach. They should not, of course, be excluded from the requirement of respecting negative responses.

California Law

As Angela Harris points out, the 1991 version of section 261 of the California Penal Code definition of forcible rape is no longer premised on assumptions about the reasonableness of the "aggressive-acquiescence" model. The revised law no longer requires that a woman physically resist her attacker. It requires only that the act be achieved by means of force, violence, danger, hardship, coercive retribution, duress, or menace. Section 261.6, which deals with consent, construes consent as "positive cooperation in act or attitude pursuant to an exercise of free will." These two sections together, Harris suggests, bring California law closer to what is reasonable from a woman's point of view.

There is one apparent problem with this law as stated. Where a man has acted without a woman's consent but without using force, it does not seem that a sexual assault would be deemed to have occurred. For the law, as Harris states it, is that forcible rape requires the use of force, or something like force, and not just the overriding of consent. But if rape is sex that is not consented to, then the law makes sense only if a show of force, or its equivalent, is the only admissible evidence of lack of consent. But this leads very quickly to the old problem—namely, that the measure of the force used will be the level of resistance offered by the woman, and that this in turn will be measured by the damage done to the woman. It would seem that this problem could be avoided by the stipulation that where there is evidence of lack of consent a rape has occurred, even where there is no evidence of force used.

As we know, there is, in many date rapes, no evidence of use of force. The simple reason is that the woman didn't resist hard enough, or perhaps, apart from her negative verbal responses, she didn't resist at all. Consider, for example, the case of a disabled woman confined to a wheelchair. It is easy to imagine how such a woman, especially one who is not very strong, might be assaulted without very much force being used.[2] In failing to provide a definition of consent that is dependent simply on the expression of negative words and gestures, and in linking the evidence of consent to the evidence of force used, the California law falls short in its ability to protect women who are really not very strong physically. I think this is wrong. What follows is a further defense of the argument for keeping the criteria separate.

Changing Paradigms

In "Date Rape: A Feminist Analysis," I argued that a model of "communicative sexuality" should be used to determine what constitutes sexual assault. This model was opposed to the prevailing model of forceful seduction, a model which has been used by the courts and is still being used in most jurisdictions. What marks the forceful-seduction model is that the negative responses women express when they are subjected to sexual pressure are not taken seriously. I argued that the nature of consent based on the communicative model is more ongoing, more tentative, more reversible than the one-shot affair envisioned on the forceful-seduction model of sexuality. On the forceful-seduction model, consent to a caress can be construed as consent to intercourse. On the alternative communicative model, partners must check up as they go along to ensure that different kinds of sexual activity are welcome. Partners may not assume that consent at the stage of kissing, for example, creates a carte blanche for intercourse, anal penetration, group sex, and bondage. Second, I maintained that the reasonableness of presuming a communicative model of sexual interaction is particularly reflective of what is reasonable from a woman's point of view, since it is the approach to adopt if women are to achieve the usual aims of sexual activity—namely, sexual pleasure and sat-

---

2. Data show that up to 80 percent of women with disabilities are the victims of sexual assault. See the study commissioned by the Ministry of Community and Social Services, Ontario, Canada, by DAWN—the DisAbled Women's Network—in 1987.

isfaction. Last, I argued in my article that this is the best model to adopt from a feminist point of view. It is best intuitively speaking because it reflects a noncoercive approach to interpersonal relations that is respectful of the person, and it is best in terms of outcome because it yields a criterion for consent that captures a higher percentage of the cases that feminists tend to think ought to be included under sexual assault.

Many applauded this rethinking of the criterion of consent. Others were clearly disturbed by it. Chords were struck, having to do with talking about sex, with what women are like, with what is fair to men, with what is practical.

Catharine Wells, for example, claims that the belief that a criterion of communicative sexuality can be used as a standard for the legal protection of women is utopian. She charges that my argument overlooks the reality of power relations between men and women. She believes that my theory remains unrooted in practice. She expresses skepticism that the point of view on which it is based is either a "woman's" point of view or feminist, and she is equally skeptical about the propriety of adopting such a stance, if indeed it exists. She believes that adopting a criterion of communicative sexuality may be unfair to men, that the points of view of men and women should be given equal time, and that there may be a general point of view which is neither male nor feminist, and which on account of its nonpartisan nature ought to be adopted.

Angela Harris shares Wells's concern about the fairness to men of taking a woman's point of view, and expresses concern that adopting a criterion of communicative sexuality may result in the conviction of the criminally innocent. She also shares Wells's reservations about the possibility of changing the social practices which issue in date rape, drawing attention to the importance of changing not just the law but also social attitudes and practices. The skepticism about change implicit in her reservations suggests that she shares Wells's view that my conclusions are utopian.

David Adams also expresses uncertainty over how the communicative model is to be implemented. He focuses on the problems that arise when a given set of words and actions generate different interpretations. He raises the philosophical question of how we are to read meanings and what gives one meaning more validity than another. In addition, he raises concerns about the authenticity of women's desires, echoing Catharine MacKinnon's concerns about the very possibility that women who have been the victims of certain well-known types of oppression are capable of consenting based on their genuine and known desires.

The questions raised by Adams, Harris, and Wells are indicative of the extreme difficulties involved when paradigms are shifted and there are no conventional and internalized answers to fall back upon. However, they take place against a background of legal change that is strongly indicative of practical solutions to the issues raised. Legal and policy changes, however, are not the end of the story, even when they result in optimal solutions from the standpoint of women and feminism. In order to work, they must be accepted by the larger society, and in order for that to happen the larger society must be able to understand why the solutions adopted have been adopted, and why they pay off, and for whom.

I propose to begin to provide a deeper understanding of why we should take communicative sexuality as a model for noncoercive sexual relations by sketching some of the theoretical and philosophical underpinnings of the argument for doing this. Only in this way can the appropriate meanings be attached to the claims I made in my original article. Only by explaining what I take the rudiments of feminist theory to be can I explain why the arguments I give are feminist. Only by explaining what certain feminist theories are saying about women can I explain why I claim to have adopted a "woman's" point of view. Only by setting out a criterion of reasonableness can I explain why I think a woman's point of view is reasonable. Only by calling on a theory of meaning can I explain why different models make a difference to the meaning of "consent." From such theories, answers to a myriad of questions about the model itself will flow: What exactly is communicative sexuality? Does it require "checking up" as you go along? Does it provide necessary and sufficient conditions for determining when sexual assault has occurred? Is the criterion of communicative sexuality too broad for assessing sexual assault? Is it too narrow? Can sadomasochistic sex be communicative? Is communicative sexuality culturally relative? Would legislation that makes communicative sexuality an essential element of consent hold men to too high a standard of epistemic responsibility? Can the required changes be made by means of the law alone? Should a high standard of communicative sexuality be required by law?

I begin with an account of the rudiments of the feminist theory on which my answers to these questions depend.

What Makes a Theory Feminist?

There is still much uncertainty concerning what constitutes a feminist theory. One reason is that there are many such theories. Different schools of feminism accept different assumptions, adopt different methodologies, and subscribe to different politics. For this reason, the Marxist feminism of Catharine MacKinnon is quite different from the liberal feminism of Bertha Wilson.[3] However, I cannot canvass all the different approaches to feminist theory here. Rather, I will touch on the essential points of a feminist approach which I have adopted, and which inform the particular solution offered in "Date Rape."

According to feminist theory, as I understand it, all known present-day societies are patriarchal. "Patriarchy" designates a type of power structure, and the theory describes power in terms of what group of people holds the preponderance of economic resources and political influence. In more concrete terms, this comes down to who owns the property; who earns the income; and who holds the high-level policy-making and decision-making positions in financial institutions, legal institutions, legislatures, universities, major corporations, and the like. According to this criterion, men everywhere have far more power than women, and this is what makes societies everywhere patriarchal.

Feminists object that the power which resides in economies, politics, and institutions is legitimized, upheld, and maintained by a kind of thinking that is more characteristic of men than it is of women. Put simply, the feminist concern is that policy made by men will primarily reflect the interests of men, or at least the interests of men as men have defined them (leaving open the possibility that the interests of men are better served when feminist agendas are met). What is widely maintained by feminists, however, is that

3. Bertha Wilson was a judge of the Supreme Court of Canada who is especially noted for her reasoning in finding the Criminal Code provision restricting abortion a violation of the constitutional right to security of person. The provision was struck down. Canada presently has no law restricting access to abortion. See *R. v. Morgentaler,* 31 CRR at 78; Catharine MacKinnon, *Toward a Feminist Theory of the State* (Cambridge: Harvard University Press, 1989).

policies developed to serve the interests of men, as men have defined them, do not further the interests of women and are often detrimental to those interests. The ways in which these interests have been played out in the case of sexual assault are thought to exemplify this point. Of course, this view presupposes that men and women have some fundamentally different interests.

The main reason for the different interests that men and women tend to have, according to prevailing feminist thinking, stems from the sexual division of labor. The division of labor is such that women do most of the reproductive labor and most of the emotional work involved in maintaining relationships. This kind of work interacts, within the power relations of patriarchy, with the conceptual schemes those power relations support. They in turn operate in relation to the body structure of women, to produce the gender "woman."

Numerous studies indicate that the typical personality structures, ways of speaking, ways of relating and ways of problem-solving of women are significantly different from those which are typical of men.[4] To the extent that this is both true and tied up in the economy of the sexual division of labor, it is possible to speak of the different interests of different genders. We are thus able to designate "a woman's interest," in one sense, as "the interest of anyone who has undertaken the reproductive responsibilities typically delegated to women within patriarchy."

Studies indicate that women are far more likely than men to interact in a communicative fashion and to work out cooperative solutions to problems. Men, in contrast, like to impose solutions that they have worked out ahead of time without recourse to extensive consultation. Women, studies show, tend to fuse sex and emotion in ways that make sexual satisfaction vastly less likely wherever a communicative approach is lacking. In addition to being more likely to fuse sexual and emotional feelings, women are more reliant on trust for good sex and have more at stake in having "unsafe sex" with a man. Men have a strong tendency to separate sexual feelings and emotional feelings and to act on the basis of the

4. See Carol Gilligan, *In a Different Voice* (Cambridge: Harvard University Press, 1982); Nancy Chodorow, "Feminine Personality and Family Structure," in *Woman, Culture, and Society,* ed. Rosaldo and Lamphere (Stanford, Calif.: Stanford University Press, 1974); Luce Irigaray, *Speculum of the Other Woman* (Ithaca, N.Y.: Cornell University Press, 1985).

former even when the latter are lacking. Men have considerably less fear of pregnancy. Women, as anyone may note, are under almost no macho pressure to have sex, and as a rule tend to be less concerned with "scoring" than men. Men are under considerable macho pressure to have sex. There is evidence, as well, that women's sexuality is more complex than men's, less transparent. As a consequence, women are less likely to get sexual satisfaction from their partners unless they convey to them their particular needs.

There have been convincing arguments to the effect that the impact of patriarchy on the structure of feminine personality is tied up with a conceptual scheme in terms of which "man" and "woman" are understood, and that this conceptual scheme is linked to gut-level responses that largely determine our fears and desires concerning "men" and "women." The significance of this cannot be understated. A powerful psychological tendency that sorts the polarities soft/hard, emotional/rational, frivolous/serious, dependent/autonomous, nature/culture, pink/blue, tender/tough, under the categories of woman/man, in defiance of all rational argument to the contrary, reveals the true nature of a conceptual scheme as an organization of the language upheld by a strong psychological investment. It indicates the extent to which the *rethinking* of gender relations often requires not just the overturning of traditional categories, but also the considerable effort of rethinking the implications of this upset and of bringing our psychological dispositions into tune with our new conclusions. Thus, in reconceptualizing traditional relationships, feminists cannot expect instant acceptance. The process must be expected to be slow, a struggle which often has to await a new generation to make significant gains.

But how, given the acknowledgment that what constitutes "woman" must be rethought, can feminists presume to take the point of view of women? One answer is that they cannot. But if they cannot, is taking the point of view of a woman a mere euphemism for an attempt to rethink the category under the feminist banner?

This answer is partly correct. The concept of woman is in flux, as is, arguably, the "nature" of women themselves. It may well be that most women of the 1990s are not like most women of the 1950s, or of the 1890s. Arguably, they have different expectations, different body images, and different self-images. Seeing themselves differently, they in many respects behave differently. More are perhaps more "male-identified." Many adopt values which have been traditionally male, focusing their main activities on competing in the marketplace, following a career track, or becoming rich and powerful. Some adopt prevailing male values about the separation of sex and emotion, sex and commitment. Some have many lovers, and a "love'em and leave'em" approach. On the other hand, there is also evidence that these differences among women have always existed. Thus, we may be on firmer ground if we argue that to the extent that "women" have changed, under the influence of the consumer individualism of the twentieth century, under the influence of the sexual revolution, under the influence of the rethinking of conceptual categories and the redefining of gender roles, the change is statistical.

Some hold that changing the concept of "woman" and redefining the gender roles played by women will actually have the effect of changing women's nature. Others take this talk to suggest a substratum "woman" of some sort, an essential woman who has thrown off patriarchal ideology and its requirements, a basic material that underlies the patriarchal dye. Thus, rather than seeing "woman" as nonessential and subject to change and "evolution," some suspect the change will be from a distorted, unnatural, artificially constrained woman to one who is as nature made her before patriarchy got ahold of her. This woman is generally portrayed as strong, powerful, loving, sexual, and knowing, particularly with respect to her own desires.

The very idea that there is an "essential woman" to be uncovered causes considerable consternation in certain political circles. The reason is understandable. Essentialist theories have been used against women in the past. They have been taken to imply that there is something unchangeable and intractable in women's nature that makes women unsuitable to participate fully in the activities of men. The belief that women have no essential traits, and hence may change, is, predictably, tied to the belief that they are flexible enough to make themselves over, when the need arises, in order to compete effectively in the marketplace, and hence to maintain equality. Hence, to pronounce that women are "one way" is to pose the danger of an ideology that will induce women to accept themselves as being less than they are, that will induce them to maintain a false self, and thus to undermine the self which is the only reliable source of power and happiness in the world. I take it that this is the danger Catharine Wells fears in my presuming to take a "woman's point of view." This is a concern I share.

I rather doubt that there is either an essential woman or an essential man. The fact that there are so many intragender differences in character traits argues against this, as does the fact of significant cross-gender overlap. Even if there is genetically produced material that programs the development of men and women in statistically significant different ways, there is no evidence that all women, or all men, have anything like the same program, or that they never share similar ones. There is no need, however, to decide the biological question. Even where we assume that all differences are culturally produced, we must acknowledge that culturally produced traits are in many cases as intractable, at least from the standpoint of short-term change, as biologically produced ones. The fact that any particular aspect of culture may change shows it is not essential. However, the attitudes and beliefs which culture produces in a particular person may, for all effects and purposes, seem essential. Thus, if it is a cultural fact that women do 90 percent of the housework, policy aimed at producing greater equality for women may aim at accommodating that fact, in the short term, for the simple reason that attempting to change it may not be effective in the short term. Similarly, if 90 percent of women have a gender structure that makes them prefer a communicative approach to sexual activity, then this cultural fact is a strong reason for accommodating that preference.

It is necessary to walk a thin line between acknowledging the cultural and biological differences that define women's reality, and that demarcate and distinguish that reality from that of men's, and describing that reality in such a way as to produce yet another ideology of "what women are like." This is especially true in matters of sexuality, since Wells is right that women's sexual nature admits of infinite variety. Her concern is that public acceptance of a particular description of one approach to sexuality might have a damaging effect on women who find that their own sexuality compares unfavorably to the standard set up. It is largely on this point of my presuming to speak about the nature of women's sexuality, and what is reasonable from her point of view, that Wells bases her charge of utopianism. This charge is tied to her accusation that I have no right to represent my position as "a woman's point of view." However, while the issues she raises are important, I find her own charges to be reactive and triggered by catch phrases. I do not find that they are based on a considered view of the issues at hand.

Utopianism and the Ideology of Forceful Seduction

Catharine Wells has charged that the hope of adopting a paradigm of communicative sexuality is utopian. This issue touches on a number of points, one of which was also addressed by Angela Harris. The concern is twofold. First, it is feared that just talking, just theorizing, won't change anything for the better. Second—and this is Harris's concern—it is feared that social intransigence will undermine any actual legal changes that are made. Wells states that this is because my analysis misses the boat. It is not rooted in social reality. It is not rooted in praxis.

Wells's claim that my analysis is not rooted in social reality refers in part to the Harlequin romance, a medium increasingly recognized as providing pornography for women, a world in which the forceful-seduction model of sexual surrender abounds. My alleged lack of realism lies in a failure to appreciate the extent to which some women fantasize about the forceful seductions which are the stock-in-trade of Harlequins. Her charge suggests that she sees these fantasies as too deeply rooted, too accepted at an ideological level, to be eradicated. But it suggests as well a radical liberalism which holds that freedom includes the right to indulge in every private taste, just so long as the only risk of harm is to oneself. On this view, the law unjustifiably interferes with one's freedom if it prohibits actions based on the wish to be murdered, or to sell oneself into slavery.

There is no doubt that the Harlequin romance and its derivatives model their pseudo-sexual encounters on a forceful-seduction model. In them, powerful inarticulate strangers override the heroine's reservations. His pressing desire for her causes her to have overwhelming erotic sensations which make it impossible for her to resist his kiss, and his kiss sends her into an even deeper spin. She begins by resisting the kiss but, after the kiss, knows it is he she will marry. Thus, ultimately eros is permitted in an atmosphere of love, trust, and impending marriage. The kiss, won after many icy reproofs on her part, becomes a mark of her ultimate value, of how much she is desired, and she wins with that kiss protestations of love until death do they part.

It is easy to see how a woman dominated by such an image could mislead a man. She believes his kiss is proof of his undying love and melts in his arms. He takes this as a positive sign that she wants to have coitus and begins to remove her clothing.[5]

But here the scene changes. She expects the respect due to a future wife and mother. He sees her as a hot number. She says "no," just as she did to the kiss, initially. He believes she will soon be overwhelmed and submit, especially once he is inside her. She struggles and protests verbally. He ignores her and rapes her.

Feminist criticism, without exception, rejects this ideology of romance. Porn for women, feminist criticism acknowledges, like porn for men, is equally offensive in its portrayal of women. Feminists analyzing the text look for the anomalies between the fantasies provided there and the reality of women who buy these fantasies.[6]

Despite the sales record of Harlequins, feminists note, most women do not want to be kissed by the wrong person, against their will, and their resistance to being kissed is not token but real. While the heroine in the story may welcome a masterful approach to being kissed, she does not welcome a masterful approach to having coitus. So the most prevalent popular imagery of women's erotica is not an imagery that includes coitus, or even sexual touching. It goes no further than the kiss and a few caresses.[7] Thus, while the masterful-seduction model of an erotic encounter offered up by cheap romance stories might seem to indicate that some women want forceful seduction leading to coitus, the analogy breaks down on every point that goes beyond kissing and stops

5. Deborah Tannen, *You Just Don't Understand* (New York: Morrow, 1990); Barrie Thorne and Nancy Henley, eds., *Language and Sex: Difference and Dominance* (Rowley, Mass.: Newbury House, 1975).

6. Ann Barr Snitow, "Mass Market Romance: Pornography for Women Is Different," in *Powers of Desire: The Politics of Sexuality,* ed. Ann Snitow, Christine Stansell, and Sharon Thompson (New York: Monthly Review Press, 1983).

7. There is innuendo in more-recent Harlequins that heroines are induced into bed, but only once the questions of undying love and marriage have been settled.

short of marriage. Moreover the handsome powerful stranger in the romance seldom is to be found in reality, so the incidence of desire for masterful seduction leading to a kiss is bound to be fairly low. The handsome stranger, moreover, does not succeed on the first date. He must pursue his quarry for a suitably long period of time and prove his desire in a number of ways prior to the kiss. Last, the model in question leads only to a kiss, and in fact seldom leads to sexual touching or to coitus. Thus, if there are some women who want their reservations overcome, that desire will apply not to all men but only to the "right one." The question of what should be their legal position remains, and of what, in light of that position, is a prudent approach for men who do not want to be charged with sexual assault for stealing a kiss.

It seems to me that the position of the woman who wants to be kissed despite her reservations is precisely the same as that of the fictional woman who wants to be raped. She will just have to hope that exactly the right man is willing to break the law and take the chance that she won't charge him with sexual assault. Obviously, if a man assaults her and she doesn't complain, nothing is going to happen. But if a man assaults her and she does complain, as she probably will if he's not the right man, then he will get into trouble, and so he should.

A better approach to a man's persistent effort to obtain a kiss is to be clear. The prospective lover can be told she doesn't want to be kissed. He can be told gently or firmly. A woman can ask for time to decide, or tell him "Not on your life!" If she is insincere, then we must keep in mind that she is the loser as well as he. But isn't this the reasonable cost of the freedom, of the self-determination, so valued as to be protected at the constitutional level in both the United States and Canada?

The issue is resolved, in my mind, by understanding that the satisfaction of every kind of sexual fantasy is compatible with communicative sexuality. The emphasis is on "fantasy." That is, we can draw a distinction between engaging in nonconsensual sex, and fantasizing and playing out engaging in nonconsensual sex. The former is illegal. The latter is legal. What makes the difference is consent itself. Where one is very clear ahead of time that one agrees to, say, bondage, forceful sex, and even some form of pain, and one is clear on how to end the game and on what is going to count as refusal in the course of the game, then under those circumstances forced sex will satisfy the communicative model. If those circumstances are lacking, then I do not know how a decision to play out a fantasy of forced sex would be distinguishable from actual forced sex in the face of actual refusal. This idea will be explored more fully below.

But in what sense is the world of the Harlequin romance rooted in reality? And how can the legal changes based on a model of communicative sexuality make an equal claim to such roots?

It is always difficult to speak of the way social reality diverges from the ideologies which attempt to account for it, for those ideologies are, at one level, part of that very same social reality. What people think, and what they will accept based on what they think, are both quite real. And ideologies themselves encourage the practices which make them look true. When people believe there are witches, they are apt to extract the confessions which confirm those beliefs. When they believe that women are less intelligent, they are apt to leave them less educated, and thus produce women who really do seem less intelligent. If it is believed that women do not like sex, many women will learn not to like it. Similarly, if it is believed that women really *like* forceful sex, and if the only kind of sex offered is of that sort, women may indeed do what they can to acquire a taste for it.

For there is no evidence that women are less susceptible to ideological persuasion than men. Even though women have been the victims of all these ideologies, they have been just as inclined to believe in witches, in their own inferiority, in romantic illusions, and in forceful seduction as men have been. Unfortunately, there are unfortunate consequences of false beliefs. False beliefs about witches resulted in the execution of innocent women. False beliefs about the merits of bleeding inflicted greater weakness and suffering on the ill and dying. The consequences of the false belief in the erotic appeal of forceful seduction are not so readily admitted. One fairly evident consequence is a high level of frustration and frigidity among women, who, unable to act on their own desires, have never been able to follow the full course of those desires. Another is the extent to which these paradigms of forceful seduction support a macho culture which is generally intimidating to women, which places heavy constraints on their freedom to travel alone, to talk to strangers, and to interact safely in the public arena.

The reality of the ideology perpetrated by Harlequin romance has, as we know, been strongly opposed by the reality of new conceptions of women, often powerfully expressed through different life-styles. By living differently, by loving differently, by being different, feminist thinking has founded, in reality, its own opposing reality. It is here that the ideal of communicative sex has been instituted and developed, and it is here that it will continue to be nurtured while society ever so slowly comes to accept its main precepts. If we are liberals, we believe that eventually the most reasonable and most truthful views will prevail, and we will keep the reasonable and the truthful alive in the hope that it will prevail at the first ripe opportunity. If we are not liberals, we can do nothing but hope. But this too is a reason for keeping the faith.

What Is Praxis?

To relate theory to praxis is just to come up with a theory that can be effectively implemented, which is to say that when it is implemented it is likely to work more or less along the lines anticipated. Social reality, on the other hand, one would think, would draw upon something that actually does take place, is already in existence.

The romance industry clearly is part of social reality, just as the pornography industry is, just as legal misconceptions about sexual assault are. It is obvious indeed that every way of living, as well as every way of thinking, is part of social reality. People who practice communicative sex are part of that reality, just as people who don't. But what these differences in social reality show is that social reality is not fixed, that it can change. What I have argued for is change, and that argument relies on the claim that some social realities are preferable to others. A social reality of comfort is preferable to a social reality of poverty; a social reality of peace is preferable to one of war; a society that practices consensual sex is preferable to one that practices rape. It is hard to see how an argument for change, which is based on what is the case and which argues as an alternative something else which is also the case, is not based on social reality.

For a theory to be related to praxis, however, it is not necessary that it be possible to implement it immediately in any society whatsoever. On the contrary, it is clear that much depends upon social climate. What may be implemented by a progressive judiciary will not be implemented by a conservative judiciary. However, a position that has been worked out ahead of time, and judged to be coherent, can contribute to the development of a more progressive judiciary. At the same time, it may be a resource that an increasingly progressive judiciary can use. But it is *practical* both to contribute to the production of a more progressive judiciary and to provide it with resources. For what is practical, in any social context, has as much to do with what people are prepared to think as with what is possible from the standpoint of physics. As has been pointed out, unless people are prepared to think about things differently, there is little hope for substantial legal change. All the more reason, then, to argue for a different point of view. One must not give up the argument, on the grounds that not enough people think that way or that some people don't. If the argument is to be given up, it must be for reasons that are internal to the argument itself and not because it is unpopular.

Feminist activism is not monolithic. It advances simultaneously on many fronts. What is thought in law is also thought in education, philosophy, psychology, history, medicine, community politics, government offices, labor unions, boards, and sorority and fraternity houses. Feminist activism has, in other words, a wide public forum. Indeed, probably no recent issue has so exercised the public imagination. Insofar as many of the people who think are also in a position to act, such thinking is highly practical. Unlike discussions of how many angels can dance on the head of a pin, feminist thinking addresses issues for which the public is actively seeking solutions. In this important respect it is not mere abstraction; it is not unrelated to practice; it is not utopian.

What then is the test that a theory may be related to praxis? One test, surely, is that it can be given a legal formulation and be enforced by the courts. We have seen that the theory I have argued for lends itself to this. The second test is that it be explainable in terms that ordinary, reasonable persons can grasp. This is essential because legal reforms may not succeed if the rationale for them is not easily grasped by the persons affected. There is ample evidence that the points underlying the drive for legal reform on date rape can be grasped at this level. Most people are capable of understanding what "no" means, what a negative response is, and what

it is to take reasonable steps to determine when consent has occurred.

Radical Freedom

The point has been raised by Catharine Wells that some persons'
sex lives might be frustrated by the obligation to voice their desires. Wells's concern is with the importance of self-determination,
particularly in what is widely regarded as the sacrosanct "private"
realm of sexual activity. The problem, as she sees it, is that a standard of communicative sex that offers greater protection for some
women might have the effect of violating the basic rights of other
persons.

In answering this concern, it helps to look at the general way in
which the law functions to protect rights. There are two functions
to note. The first is the way in which the protection of negative
rights may suffice to protect positive rights, without the latter
being given any independent guarantees. The second is the necessity of arriving at the proper conception of rights by means of a
trade-off of interests, some of which trump others.

Criminal law in particular protects what we call negative rights:
the right not to be assaulted, robbed, murdered, defrauded, and so
on. It does not give us positive rights—for instance, the right to
money, jobs, sexual satisfaction, and happiness. The liberal theory
on which it is based supposes that in protecting negative rights the
criminal law provides people with a concomitant positive right to
pursue the goals and to seek the commodities and pleasures that
will make them happy. Thus, in protecting us from robbery the
law frees us to seek the accumulation of wealth. By analogy, by
protecting us from sexual assault, the law leaves us free to find and
enjoy sexual pleasure.

However, there are logical limits on what positive rights can be
protected. The desire to be murdered by one's best friend is not a
positive right that can be provided for by the law against murder.
Neither can the desire to be sold into slavery be accommodated by
the law against slavery, nor can the desire to be battered without
one's consent be accommodated by the law against battery. These
are the paradoxes of freedom which emerge at the conceptual lim-

its of the freedoms secured by law. A great deal has been written in an effort to resolve the paradoxes.[8]

A common strategy is to locate the rationale for these limits in a substantive understanding of the truly free individual. A truly free individual cannot want to be a slave or to die or to have his or her bodily integrity infringed upon, because all these things destroy the very freedom which makes him a valuable individual worthy of the law's protection. Basically the same argument can be fallen back on with respect to the woman who does not want the law to protect her from nonconsensual sex. In protecting such a woman, the law protects her freedom to have sex only when she wishes to. In failing to offer this protection, it undermines the substantial freedom that lies in retaining this option, as well as the freedom that would be lost on those occasions when she really was forced against her will.

A second strategy is to recognize the fact that legislation that creates positive rights must be balanced against the interests of most people in having their negative rights protected. Typically, in making legislation, legislators must pit individual interests against the need to protect the public interest, against the interests of the state, and against the private interests of other individuals. Where public interests are significant, minor curtailments of individual freedoms are usually regarded as justified. This is clearly true in the case of seat-belt legislation. Most people agree that if legislating the wearing of seat belts is a good way to save the lives of significant numbers of persons, and thereby ensure that they continue to pay their taxes, parent their children, and exercise their skills, the interests of a few people who would prefer to risk death and disability rather than to suffer the irritation of having to wear a seat belt have to be sacrificed. This is not to say, either, that those who refuse to wear seat belts will be forced to wear them. It is to say, rather, that if they don't wear them and they get caught, they will have to pay a penalty.

Thus, one thing which makes legislation reasonable is precisely the fact that it provides significant protection of the public interest

8. Richard Hare, "What Is Wrong with Slavery?" *Philosophy and Public Affairs* 8 (1979), 103–21; Joel Feinberg, *Harm to Self* (New York: Oxford University Press, 1986), 71.

at a relatively insignificant cost. The situation involved in protecting women from sexual assault is analogous. If, as a matter of statistical fact, legislating communication as a central component of consensual sex is a good way to protect women from being sexually assaulted, then the interest a relatively few people may have in hazarding noncommunicative sex may just have to be sacrificed. Moreover, if communication is a component of consent, it does not follow that anyone will be forced to have consensual sex. Those who don't, however, run the risk of paying the penalty. I suspect, though, that this is a specious concern and has no real application.[9]

Why Take a Woman's Point of View? Is It Fair?

The question all three commentators put is, essentially, whether it is fair to men for laws and regulations to adopt a woman's point of view. Wells puts the question in terms of whether there is a general standpoint which the law could take, one informed by neither a feminist nor a patriarchal point of view. Harris puts it more in terms of whether it is unfair to switch the rules on men, to change the terms under which they are used to working. Adams puts it in terms of which interpretation of the meaning of words, gestures, and actions should be chosen when there is one interpretation from a man's point of view and one from the female victim's point of view.

The question has an analogue in the debate on affirmative action. If men have benefited from a practice for a long time, is it now fair that women should benefit and that men should be disadvantaged? Does one injustice deserve another injustice? If men have been unfair in the past, is it now fair that women should get to be unfair?

One answer to this concern is that it is not a question of equalizing unfairness, but rather a question of changing what is unfair to

9. The very possibility of wanting nonconsensual sex presupposes a distinction between wanting sex and consenting to it. But this is not a difficult distinction to maintain. As was pointed out in "Date Rape," I may want to have sex, but refuse it on a number of grounds: for religious reasons, for health reasons, in order to avoid pregnancy. It is this distinction that allows us to say of a woman, without inconsistency, that she wants to be raped. But wanting to be raped, like wanting to be murdered by one's best friend, does not settle the issue.

something fair. The patriarchal point of view is unfair to women. The feminist point of view, however, is not unfair to men. Thus it will not be unfair to take a feminist point of view.

In assessing this answer, we should keep in mind the respective vulnerabilities of men and women. The sexual politics of date rape are clear. Women are vulnerable to force being used. Men are vulnerable to being falsely accused. Men, if they are well-meaning, will want to be sure they don't use force unintentionally. This, as I have argued, is an easily attainable goal. All they have to do is ask. The expectation that they should ask will be unfair only if men do not receive fair notice of that requirement.

There is a second concern about unfairness expressed by Harris and Adams. It is the unfairness of suddenly changing the terms on men who think that forceful seduction is what women want. If the rules are changed and men aren't informed, then, it is feared, men with innocent minds will be found guilty.

This argument, however, is hardly convincing. Whenever any law is changed, there is a danger that some ill-informed citizen will run afoul of it. However, this danger is not widely accepted as an argument against legal change. Provided that law is duly promulgated, we expect citizens to adjust their behavior to conform with the law. This expectation is indeed one of the most fundamental tenets of the legal system. It is formulated as the maxim "Ignorance of the law is no excuse." Without this principle and the principle of fair notice (that the law be promulgated), it would indeed be impossible to make legal changes fairly.

Ignoring a patriarchal point of view, it may be argued, is nonetheless justifiable only if it can be established that such a standpoint is fundamentally unfair, that it is not just one way of seeing things fairly.

In considering this objection, we must bear in mind that forceful seduction is supposed to be about what women want. So if women want something else, the belief just turns out to be false, and relatively useless. There is no point in holding onto it in the interests of fairness or anything else.

If, on the other hand, a preference for forceful seduction is actually a reflection of what men want, a desire that is then projected onto women, then it is clear that it serves men's interests while it frustrates and victimizes women. Just as clearly this cannot be fair.

It is not fair to serve the interests of thieves when serving those interests jeopardizes the safety and happiness of property owners who cannot sustain the thefts. As has already been argued, protecting the rights of those few people whose pleasure consists in being robbed cannot be justified if it is at the expense of a failure to protect the vast majority whose pleasure does not consist in being robbed.

The conclusion we should draw, then, is clear. As long as legal changes are the result of due process and given the usual coverage in the media and by government publications, it is never unfair in the sense of "unfair surprise" to change the law. Moreover, the presumption of innocence in no way depends on how the law is changed. Rules of procedure and rules of evidence have developed under common law to provide for all persons accused under any law to receive the benefit of the doubt. But if it is not unfair to change the law, and it is not unfair to dispense with an unfair point of view, then taking a feminist point of view will not constitute any kind of unfairness unless it is unfair in itself. My position, of course, is that it is not.

Reasonableness

Criticisms of my claims about "reasonableness" come from two opposing directions. One concerns the location of reasonableness in a woman's point of view. The other concerns the reasonableness of expecting real change and ties in with the charge of utopianism.

The latter concern has already been addressed. It has been answered in part by showing that both the law and interpretations of the law do change, and that in some jurisdictions they have changed in the desired direction. But if they can change in some quarters, they can change in others. There is hope.

The second question raised was whether communicative sexuality is reasonable from a "woman's point of view." Let me outline what I mean by "reasonable."

The location of reasonableness within a woman's interest in obtaining good sex references a probability relationship between means and ends. If A represents good sex, and B represents a probable means to achieving A, and there are no other equally probable means to *A*, then we may conclude that any reasonable person who wishes *A* will adopt *B*.

As already noted, the conclusion that communicative sex is reasonable from a woman's point of view is based on gender studies which conclude that, by and large, women's sexuality is physically more complex than men's, that men are often less than knowledgeable about women's sexuality, and that women are unlikely to obtain sexual satisfaction when a communicative approach is lacking.

Although there is some evidence that men have better sex if they engage in communicative sex, so that communicative sex would be reasonable from their point of view as well, there is also evidence that they can get "good enough" sex without it. There may be biological reasons for this. Other reasons are clearly social. There is strong evidence that men tend to keep their emotional needs separate from their sexual needs, or at least that they don't integrate those needs as well. It is unquestionable, as well, that men are under the influence of strong macho imperatives to have sex, and that many men believe they have strong sexual appetites that require satisfaction. Still others associate having sex with punishment and the exercise of power; strong evidence of the existence of this association is to be found in the relationship between war and rape. Since sex, for many men, is a matter of "scoring" or "getting lucky," they are apt to see sexual interplay as a kind of war game, and sex as a kind of conquest to which they are entitled when women either break the rules or succumb to their strategies. If they (women) wear the wrong clothes, or are too trusting, or foolishly go to a man's apartment, or have too many drinks, then the women lose the game and are, as it were, fair game. All this, if true, shows that what is reasonable from a man's point of view is quite different from what is reasonable from a woman's point of view.

There are three ways in which this second claim about reasonableness of communicative sex from a woman's point of view can be challenged. The first is to challenge the factual claim that communicative sex is more likely to lead to sexual satisfaction than, say, good luck. This challenge seems implausible. Indeed, even someone who was extremely lucky in both love and sex would be bound to have her luck enhanced just in case she could communicate her needs. Even someone who wished to experience erotic sensations in an extremely passive and silent state would fare better if she could communicate that desire to her partner. In fact, successful strategies in obtaining the last sort of sex may involve more communication than that required for less exotic kinds of taste. Moreover, passive, silent sex *is* consistent with not registering a negative response, and indeed with giving a positive response to a sincere inquiry. The only other possibility I can think of is someone who can generate good sex for herself, out of her own body and imagination, independently of anything that is offered to her by her partner. However, it seems to me that where someone's sexual experience could be spoiled by interference from another person, a proper discussion of that fact early on is one good way to prevent such interference.

The second challenge is not so much a challenge as a change in the terms of reference. It supposes that having good sex is not always the main goal in agreeing to engage in sexual activity. Women may have sex in order to please their partners, in order to get pregnant, or because they believe it is their duty. And it seems clear that they are perfectly entitled to engage in sex for these reasons. This shows, it is thought, that what is reasonable for one woman is not necessarily reasonable for another, and that there is therefore no universally reasonable point of view.

I concede both these points. If one is not concerned with having good sex, engaging in communicative sex is not going to be a reasonable means to any defined goal. However, if we are concerned that women who do not want to have good sex do not get assaulted against their will, it is still reasonable to ground a criterion of consent in the basic requirements of communication.

A third challenge is to deny "la difference." Sometimes these denials are based on strenuous attempts to be different, to show that women, or men, do not satisfy the despicable stereotypes. Sometimes, we may presume, these efforts succeed. However, denial of what is the case does not make it any less the case.

I believe that the vast majority of women have a greater need for communicative sex, even to have "good enough" sex, than most men, and this is the basis of my claim that communicative sex is reasonable from a women's point of view. It does not matter if there are exceptions to this claim. If at this point in our cultural and historical development it is true for the vast majority of women, that is all I need.

The Problem of Cultural Difference

Wells raises the point that in presuming to take a "woman's point of view" I do not speak for women in all cultures and classes. I confess that I am unsure what the point of this objection is, and I believe that most of the issues underlying it have already been dealt with. I have already conceded that not all women will have the same interests or goals. However, I see no reason to be overly concerned about this point. It seems to me that if there is a genuine cultural objection to a specific point it should be stated and we should think about it seriously. However, general allegations that "someone might have a different point of view" do nothing to advance our thinking on the subject.

That being said, it may be allowed that there are cultures in which it would be shocking for a woman to give any positive expression to her desire. In fact, it is my impression that the culture of white, educated women of European descent was much like that until fairly recently.

For such a woman, a communicative requirement which required her to volunteer positive expression to her desire may not be reasonable—in fact, it might be embarrassing and shame-inducing. However, I cannot believe that there are cultures in which women may not express their opposition to having sex with acquaintances, friends, and strangers. Perhaps those who are concerned with this possibility could give an example, accompanied by some convincing evidence.

In any case, sensitivity to cultural difference does not imply that all legislation and administration of justice must respect that difference. We do not need to make clitoridectomy legal because some cultures practice it, any more than we need to restrict women's movements because some cultures do. The context of my claim to examine a woman's point of view is, clearly, then, a liberal democratic society which espouses the equality of women and which holds liberal attitudes toward sex and toward women's entitlement to sex.

Feminism and "A Woman's Point of View"

The explanation of feminism and of "a woman's point of view" just presented enables me to answer three questions raised by Catharine Wells. The first is in what sense my position is a feminist one; the second is whether it is correct to describe it as representing a woman's point of view; the third is whether taking a woman's point of view implies essentialism.

The answer to why my position is feminist is, I believe, fairly straightforward. I have identified what I regard as patriarchal ideology concerning rape and sexual assault. This ideology is well documented in both social and legal thinking about rape, and is tagged not as ideology but as reality. I have done what I could to debunk the ideology, and have attempted to rethink the issues colored by that ideology. I have attempted to rethink them in ways that represent a point of view of persons, of women, who are quite different from the persons constructed by that ideology. These persons, these women, do not mince words. They want their words respected. They know their own desires at least well enough to know what they don't want. They enjoy sex more when it involves a certain level of communication with respect to what feels good and what doesn't, what is working and what is not. These persons, these women, their point of view, do exist in the world. Indeed, it is my suspicion that their view prevails. Yet the law traditionally has not even considered their point of view. To inquire what is true for women, to construct a point of view based on that truth, is a basic feminist method. To argue that society, theorists, the law, should consider those truths, those points of view, is to argue a feminist position. To present those truths is, unavoidably, to present a woman's point of view—maybe not the point of view of every woman, maybe not only a women's point of view, but certainly a woman's point of view, and also a woman's point of view that is significant and needs to be heard.

A related question is whether it is possible, in spite of the radically different tastes we might expect women to display, to delineate a position that is sufficiently general to encompass the interests of significant numbers of women. If it is, I see no reason that we should not call such a position a "woman's point of view." Such a view need not, like Rousseau's "general will," represent the interests of every woman. It suffices if it protects quite a significant number, and it represents a stronger interest to the extent that it represents the interests of the more vulnerable. Insofar as it is feminist, it must represent an interest which, from a feminist standpoint, is an interest in being better off. In the context of sexual assault, it will represent an interest in attaining more effective protection from sexual assault, something which, from a feminist perspective at least, will make most women better off.

The last question has already been answered. Both evidence and logic support the view that there is no such thing as an essentialist woman. Second, if there were, it is unlikely if it would matter. Whatever is essential about women is unlikely to make any difference in whether women should have a right to consent to sexual activity, or in what the criteria of that consent should be.

Concerns Regarding Communicative Sexuality

In addition to concerns raised about the advisability of switching our paradigms of sexual behavior from that of the forceful-seduction model to that of the communicative sexuality model, a number of questions concerning the nature of communicative sexuality, what it involves and how it functions, have been asked.

The major concerns center on the criterion and come from completely opposite directions. The first is that the standard set by the model of communicative sexuality is too high, that the definition of consent it supports is too narrow, and that as a consequence too much that is innocent could be judged culpable.

The criticism relies on two possibilities. The first, which has already been canvassed, is that some people prefer not to communicate their sexual preferences and that we shouldn't make that preference criminal. The second, which we have yet to consider, is that some people like to engage in sadomasochistic sex and that the communicative requirement makes this impossible.

The second criticism is that the standard of communicative sexuality I recommend is too low, that the definition of consent it supports is too broad, and that, as a consequence, too much that is guilty would be judged innocent. This criticism is concerned with the possibility that some women are subject to circumstances which, although they may pass the legal test for being noncoercive, are so coercive in fact that the positive unambiguous agreement of women in such circumstances should not count as consent. This criticism also suggests that my presumptions about the criterion of coercion do not take into account all possible cases of coercion and therefore may not be objective. It thus holds out, as a criterion of adequacy, the utopian goal of not leaving anything out.

The questions that are asked are roughly as follows: How are we to set the standard for communicative sexuality? What are its necessary and sufficient conditions? Why do we need a theory at all? How is the "communication" in communicative sexuality to be understood, and how are we to decide between different meanings? How is "meaning" determined?

The first two questions are raised by Angela Harris's charge that, in my view, communicative sexuality is not just a good idea but also ought to be the law. The charge is based on a quite understandable misunderstanding about my use of the communicative model of sexuality. I shall therefore begin with a discussion of this use.

How Does the Communicative Model Function?

Communicative sexuality is, very simply, a model of sexual interchange which is to be contrasted to the still ideologically dominant forceful-seduction model. The communicative model is based on an understanding of what is, for many sexually active adults, ongoing intimate conversation. The conversation involves, among other things, taking positive steps, when engaged in sexual activity, to determine how one's partner is responding. However, it is one thing to use a model of an ideal sexual conversation for the purpose of illustrating a concept. It is another thing, as Harris points out, to make that ideal the law. We certainly do not want a theory that implies that only practiced conversationalists can have consensual sex.

The ideal was not supposed to set the minimum standard of sexual exchange. Rather, it is intended to provide an effective illustration of what reciprocal sexual interest is like. To the extent that the illustration is successful, it enables us to picture things somewhat differently and to shift our expectations and our understanding accordingly. As such, it is intended to assist us in arriving at the required minimum standard of reciprocity. This minimum standard, as we shall see, does not entail that the highest level of intuitive understanding of where one's partner is be exercised. It requires only that negative responses be given their ordinary meanings, that positive steps be taken to discover whether one's partner really consents, and the acknowledgement that consent may be withdrawn at any stage during the proceedings.

Why Do We Need a Theory at All?

Catharine Wells presents the skeptical position. According to her, no theory of communicative sexuality is needed in order to yield an adequate criterion for sexual assault. She believes that it is self-evident that "no" means no and that this is all we need to understand.

This claim, however, overlooks the main problem, which is that, on the "forceful-seduction" model of sexuality, "no" does not mean no. Indeed, on that model "no" cannot mean no. If it did, the model wouldn't work.

This relationship between the model and the meaning of "no" reflects a fact which philosophers of language have long accepted—namely, that the meaning of words is theory-laden. What this means, for practical purposes, is that the meaning of a word cannot be changed unless the theory in which it is embedded is changed first. What the model of communicative sexuality does is change our theory about how sexual encounters may be expected to develop, by providing a plausible model of a sexual dynamic that is different from the "forceful-seduction" model. If we adopt the new model, it becomes a lot less likely that "no" will mean anything but no.

On the "forceful-seduction" model, erotic developments are enhanced when negative responses are treated as positive responses. Given that expectation, we have a good reason for thinking that saying "no" is sometimes a way of saying yes. However, on the communicative model the opposite is true. On that model, we expect that erotic developments will be enhanced only when negative responses have the same force as in other contexts. Thus, on the communicative model of sexual encounters we have no reason to think that "no" means yes.

The argument for a model of erotic development according to which "no" means no takes place against the prevailing belief that, in the context of the language of desire spoken by lovers, words and gestures take on different meanings, and the whole mythology of masculine aggression and feminine coyness was called in to explain why this was so. The big problem with this theory of sexual language, however, was that the mythology which accounted for it was just that, and did not adequately reflect reality. In particular, the theory did not adequately account for when "no" really did mean "no." On a larger scale, it did not allow for the possibility that women were capable of knowing their own desire and of expressing it.

Now it is logically possible to speak a secret language. Two or more people may develop a secret code, one in which "green" means "red," "black" means "white," "cow" means "dog," and so on. In such a language, "no" may very well mean "yes." But in order for such a secret code to exist, there must be some sort of prior interpersonal agreement concerning the code designation for each word. Moreover, if only some of the people who try to speak the language know what the agreements are, not everyone will be able to achieve their communicative ends. A greater danger exists where those with the most power get to decide disputed meanings in ways that serve their own interests.

There is another problem with allowing for arcane sexual languages in which meanings are indeterminate. If we allow that "no" often does not mean no, it is only reasonable to suppose that something else must. And as the history of case law on sexual assault shows, the most commonly accepted sign of refusal is physical resistance. Moreover, on the forceful seduction model, a distinction was drawn between a woman's resistance and her will. A woman who resisted a sexual advance did not necessarily submit to it against her will. For it to be against her will, the resistance had to be more than "token." Indeed, in most cases, in order for resistance to count as being "against her will," she had to resist to the "utmost." Running out of steam counted as changing her mind.

However, this requirement creates problems. Insofar as physical resistance is required, there are too many situations in which women are lost. Moreover, where "nontoken" physical resistance is the only valid expression of resistance, evidence of physical resistance is required. Unfortunately, acquiring that evidence can be dangerous, leading to bruises and cuts, broken jaws and black eyes, strangulation, and so on. Ultimately resisting to the utmost leads to the escalation of violence; ultimately it involves the hazarding of one's life. For many women, the struggle would not be worth it.

The undeniable advantage of the communicative model is that evidence of force is not required for there to be evidence of more than "token" resistance. If the evidence shows that there was a negative verbal response, or that gestures of refusal were made, that suffices to show that an act was "against her will." No further proof of assault is required.

There is another problem with the idea that a show of force is the only convincing sign of nonconsent, and I think that this problem continues to obfuscate thought about sexual assault.

Sexual activity can be vigorous. Many times it may be difficult to distinguish the energy and direction used to overcome a woman's expressed desire from the energy and direction used to satisfy her desire. From the standpoint of physical activity, rape may be indistinguishable from a kind of playful wrestling. Also, it is undeniable that many people like to play at various kinds of domination when they are having sex.

This recognition that normal communicative sex can be vigorous inclines me to disagree with Wells when she asserts, without argument, that consent is not central to issues of rape and that force is. I believe that exactly the opposite is true, that it is consent that is central, not force. If someone explicitly utters a positive request to be tied up and ravished, that is precisely what makes it consensual. Conversely, if she is tied up in opposition to her objections, she does not consent.

Notwithstanding the vigor of some people's sex lives, I think that whenever there is evidence of the use of force that amounts to more than energetic engagement, overriding evidence of uncoerced positive verbal indication that it is wanted and enjoyed is needed. At the very least, the use of any force in the face of verbal refusal should never be regarded as consensual.

Unless we define "aggressive" as "noncommunicative," so that nothing would count as aggressive unless it were noncommunicative, it remains conceptually possible that aggressive sex may be communicative. Moreover, it is important to maintain this distinction. It is precisely the possibility of taking an aggressive stance, of saying what one wants, that makes communicative sex possible.

In emphasizing this, however, I might be accused of stating in principle what could never be determined in practice. Aggression or force has always been taken as visible evidence of nonconsent. What else could count as evidence of a negative response?

This is certainly a difficult question. In answering it, I find it useful to keep firmly in mind the distinction between the question of the criterion of consent and the question of what counts as evidence for that criterion. It is important not to build an account of the second into the criterion for the first. The fact that we cannot always know what transpired in private between two people does not mean that we should not at least have a standard in mind with respect to what would count as a consensual transaction. For quite frequently we do get the correct story, and what is at issue is the interpretation of agreed-upon facts. Also, different stories are credible, depending on what our background theory is about what is reasonable. It is undeniable that if a woman brings a charge against a man and he is a good liar, it may be impossible to build a case against him. In this respect, the new criterion is not an advance on the old one. However, the model of communicative sexuality requires that different questions be asked, the answers to which must be supported by the circumstances, and in the face of these different questions it may be harder for liars to tell a credible story.

What Is Involved in Communicative Sex?

Many people find open, honest communication difficult, not because it is difficult to find words for what they have to say but because they are shy, vulnerable, or afraid of exposure, ridicule, or the humiliation of being ignored. However, not communicating carries with it too great a price. One's desires, one's preferences, cannot be respected or satisfied unless they are known. And in interpersonal situations, where there is a close connection between respecting desires and respecting basic rights, a certain minimum level of communication respecting those desires becomes necessary. However, some questions that have been asked about how communication and respecting desires are related reveal that not very much thought has been given to how this is to take place in intimate contexts.

I was quite astonished, for example, by the attempt David Adams makes to construct a counterexample to my claim that consent in intimate contexts is not a one-shot affair but an ongoing process. My concern is that Adams's point, though truly bizarre, may be an accurate reflection of where some males are, literally, when they claim to be having sex. Adams argues that if I consent to lend someone my car she isn't expected to check back every five minutes to update my consent. But it's not like that when you're having sex. When you're having sex you don't have to phone in. If I were riding with my friend in the car and I suddenly decided that I wanted my car back because I didn't like the way she was driving, I would expect her to give up the wheel. Similarly, a man in full possession of his faculties should be right on the spot. Knowing what's going on is part of the activity.

A review of how these communicative requirements can be met, and reflection on how normal and necessary they are, will set into relief the problem with ignoring communication requirements in thinking about sexual assault.

There is, first, verbal communication. Into this class I would put such standard questions, responses, and assertions as "Would you like to stay the night?" "No thanks." "Are you using anything?" "Do you have a condom?" "Leave me alone." "I don't feel like it" "Stop it!" and so on. These kinds of questions are fairly standard, and most people involved in dating are quite familiar with them.

The second kind of communication consists of responses which may be read as negative or positive. If you kiss me, and I kiss you back, that confers the strong presumption that I liked your kiss. If you try to kiss me, and I turn away, the presumption is that I don't want your kiss. If you caress me, and I throw my arms around you, you are entitled to presume I liked the caress. If you caress me, and I push you away, you should presume the opposite. If you undo one of my buttons, and I help you with the rest, you may presume that I am happy to get undressed. If you undo my button, and I try to do it back up again or clutch at the gap created, then you should assume the opposite.

To those more in the know, communication also takes place at the level of sexual responses related to levels of arousal, and people who are good at reading the signs make good lovers. Anyone who has ever read sex manuals knows the basic language involved. When a man is aroused, his penis swells and his glans penis becomes lubricated. When a woman is aroused, her vagina becomes noticeably lubricated and her labia become swollen and rigid. When her nipples are brushed, they harden. The manuals note, and most lovers know, that a certain amount of foreplay is requisite for the arousal of most women, and even if it isn't required it is normally desirable. I think there are few women who like sex who would demur on this point. So that even where things have proceeded in silence, to initiate the usual foreplay is to invite both a positive physiological response and to rule out negative verbal and physical responses. But then, where no physical response is forthcoming a verbal inquiry is in order, even where initial consent has been obtained. Where a woman does not kiss back, makes no return caress, and shows no signs of physiological arousal, the usual requirements of reciprocal sexual enjoyment are apparently not, from her point of view at least, being met. Where her partner does not care, does not take the trouble to notice, and makes no inquiry as to the motivation for this unusual behavior, this failure is even more evident. It is in this situation where a negative response on her part, or a failure to take positive steps to determine her consent on his part, makes the encounter look more like assault.

Once we understand what communicative sexuality is and how it is supposed to work, it becomes difficult to see how the hard case cited by David Adams is a hard case.

Hard Cases

David Adams cites a case in which a woman argued that she succumbed to the wishes of her assailant because the look in his eyes was threatening. By parity of reasoning, he suggests, her assailant would be entitled to read the look in her eyes as inviting. What Adams is suggesting is that communicative sex depends on the ability of potential lovers to read the looks in each other's eyes. If Adams is right, it would indeed set an impossible standard. What makes the standard possible is the fact that certain words, gestures, and acts have settled social meanings and that communicators are entitled to rely on those meanings. What makes the standard more than possible is the further possibility of implementing a policy with respect to those meanings.

Where the legal policy stipulates that negative verbal responses or gestures are to be given their normal meanings in sexual contexts, there is no need for interlocutors to "read the look in each other's eyes." If, moreover, as has happened in Canada, the courts hold that a man must take positive steps in order to determine that consent has been given, then the person who is in the position to take without asking must ask.

The first thing to point out, in rereading the hard case, even though it must be obvious, is that the meaning of a look cannot be deciphered unless it has been scanned in context. Even threatening looks are not actually threatening if a woman is on otherwise safe ground. But on ground which women and men both know is not safe, in a situation which has already involved a heavy hand and too much pressure, any male gaze not counterbalanced by sincere inquiries into what she desires and considerate responses to her answers may indeed be threatening.

In the case Adams cites, the woman said: "You can get a lot of other girls down there, for what you want," and the man "kept saying no." He did not say "If you don't want to, it's okay," which is the only response which would diffuse the threat. She said, "If I do what you want, will you let me go without killing me?" Such a question is a clear indication that she felt threatened. A man engaging in communicative sex would reassure her that he had no intention of killing her, that he was sorry she was frightened, and that if she didn't want to stay he would give her back her car keys (which he had taken) and let her go home.

In the case in question, the man put his hands on her throat, "lightly choking" her. This response can be read only as a reinforcement of her fear that he might kill her. Thus, the look in his eyes was read within a context in which she had been lured into a strange neighborhood in the middle of the night, had had her keys appropriated, and had expressed her desire that he seek someone else for his purposes and her fear that he might kill her. It is easy to see how his look could have been read as threatening. It is impossible to see how, in the context of her protests, her look could have been seen as inviting.

The case Adams cites is a clear case of noncommunicative sex in which a woman clearly expressed her terror to her assailant, and he reinforced her fears by placing his hands on her throat and insisting that no one else would do. But since the courts did not presume a norm of communicative sex, their main concern was whether force was used. Thus, debate centered on whether "light choking" was the use of force or just a heavy caress.

The victim's lack of resistance in this case was a problem. This lack was explained in terms of fear, and the debate also focused on whether the victim's fear was reasonable and whether, being reasonable, her failure to resist more strenuously could be understood. Thus, her negative responses were not enough in themselves to make the sexual encounter nonconsensual. The presumption was that she should resist as well. Her resistance would measure the extent to which force was used. This requirement of physical resistance was overruled, in the minds of some of the judges, only because they believed that the threatening situation was also a measure of force. Ultimately, however, her assailant was acquitted.[10]

Now it is abundantly clear that on the communicative model the case would not have turned on whether "light choking" constituted the use of force. Her nonconsent would have been adequately established by her initial refusal, her attempt to bargain her way out of the deal, her expression of the fear that she was going to be killed, his failure to ask a sincere question, and his failure to give credence to her negative response.

The Problem of Sadomasochism

Some people like sadomasochistic sex, and this is thought to create a problem for the model of communicative sexuality. In fact, the problem is not much different from the problem set for someone who wants to be "forcefully" seduced. From the standpoint of the court, tying someone up, whipping her, and causing other kinds of pain is evidence that an encounter is nonconsensual. It can, of course, be countered by evidence that the encounter was consensual. The essential point, again, is that not just physical resistance but also negative verbal responses count as nonconsent.

SAMOIS, a San Francisco–based lesbian sadomasochist group, has addressed this issue at some length in *Coming to Power*. The group argues that such practices can be engaged in morally only if

10. *Rusk v. State,* 43 Md. App. 476, 406 A.2d 624 (1979), reversed on appeal, 289 Md. 230, 424 A.2d 720 (1981). See Susan Estrich, *Real Rape* (Cambridge: Harvard University Press, 1987), 63–66.

a system of communication is worked out ahead of time by means of which the vulnerable partner may indicate when she has had enough. This position, so far as it goes, strikes me as unassailable in principle. In practice, the effectiveness of such a system of communication is bound to be a bit precarious. Trust that one will not be betrayed would seem to be of the essence. Thus, if a man, in particular, wishes to practice sadism on a willing woman whom he does not know very well and does not absolutely trust, it seems to me that he would do well to have her sign some sort of agreement, in which the absolute limits of the encounter, as well as what sort of signal was going to count as "no" or "I've had enough," were made clear. (One can imagine standard forms available at the local S and M bar, witnessed by the bartender.) There will still be a danger, of course. We rightly fear that signing such a form could provide a cover for too many things. Still, it may be that the practicalities of securing protection require that dominatrixes, in particular, require agreements.[11]

Knowing Her Own Desire

The second concern is that some women have been so intimidated that even their positive responses must be regarded as a product of something like extortion. Some women, it is thought, go out of their way to please men, not in order to please themselves but because they fear the consequences of being displeasing.

I do not doubt that this kind of fear, or desire, occurs, especially among women who lack an independent income, supportive family and friends, and legal recourse. It is not clear, either, that there is a legal solution to this problem, though this should not surprise us. The law cannot prevent all moral and psychological failures. It is designed to prevent only the most extreme instances of such failure, only those failures which are fundamental to a "free and democratic" body politic. Less fundamental social problems must be addressed by other means.

The best way to eliminate women's fear, in the long term, is to ensure that all women who wish to can enter the workforce and

11. I doubt that practiced, open, and committed sadomasochists would object too much. It is the sexually unpracticed who have difficulty admitting what they are up to. Signing an agreement, for the sexually open, would not be any more embarrassing than buying a condom or renting a hotel room.

produce for themselves an independent income. This is an enormous undertaking, but I can think of no other policy that is likely to work. The law can play a role by supporting equal opportunity and equal pay legislation, by enforcing child support and alimony payments, and by providing protection to women who are battered by their partners or who are subjected to sexual harassment and assault.

My Own Story

Philosophers are so often accused of doing armchair philosophy, and so of having no direct acquaintance with the subjects about which they theorize, that I cannot resist the temptation to say that here I have had experience.

Firsthand testimony has its limitations. It is a fallacy to generalize on the basis of one's own case, and this is the fallacy attributed to persons who take their own perspective to be the universal one. However, to the extent that one is a typical product of a typical culture, a personal testimony may provide insight into a more widespread phenomenon. It may help us to understand the factors that produce typical behaviors. Insofar as such an experience is different, it provides a standard against which other experiences may be compared. Insofar as the experience is *my* experience, it may reveal the limits of my own epistemological standpoint, and thus aid my readers in their critical assessments of my theory. It may also provide the reader with some reassurance that the abstractions which take as their starting points established legal positions can be related to someone's actual experiences.

I am a Canadian. I am becoming sort of middle-class, now that I am an academic, but I'm not sure I'll ever really feel middle class. I once wrote a poem called "I Hate the Working-Class" in which I expressed the love-hate relationship I had toward the rather rough world in which I was reared. It was a world of considerable violence, much of which was directed toward me and some of which was directed by me. I do not know to what extent all worlds are like this. I do not know if it was this world, or my Irish family, which spawned in me the righteous indignation I have so often tapped in my own defense. I do not know how many women have my capacity for anger, or my talent for giving it poignant verbal expression at just the right times.

I have always said that I have never been raped. This is true because every time someone tried to rape me I threatened with such murderous intent to ruin his entire life that he believed me, gave up in disgust, and went off in a bad temper. I will now describe some of these attempts.

On several occasions I was physically attacked, thrown on the floor or dragged into a bedroom, pinned down, kisses and caresses attempted, and ample body contact made. In none of these cases would there have been any point in physical resistance. Although I am quite strong for a woman, I was in each case quickly and completely immobilized. Perhaps because I "sort of knew the person" and was not particularly wary, I was taken by surprise. Although force was clearly used, it was so effective that it left no signs at all. One second I was on my feet; the next second I was on the floor or the bed. There was no doubt about the intent of these attacks. My assailants always informed me in a clear, quiet voice that I was going to be raped. I really had the impression that they took great pleasure in saying that. In one case, I was not physically attacked but was told by four moving-men who had just delivered my furniture that they were going to rape me.

My defense was always the same. To the men who promised to rape me I promised in return that if they did I would make the rest of their lives a living hell. I went into graphic detail. The graphic detail always included attacking them with a hammer while they were sleeping, knocking them unconscious, and cutting off their testicles. I made it clear I would not fear any consequence in seeking my revenge. In each case I was believed, and I know I would not have been believed if I had not meant every threat I uttered. I was, of course, very fortunate that none of my assailants was a murderer as well as a rapist. Thus, I persuaded each of my assailants to change his mind, and in my own mind constructed my experiences as experiences in which I had not been raped. It never occurred to me, until years later, that these attempts at rape constituted sexual assaults. Thus, in saying I had never been raped I left out the fact that I was sexually assaulted at least twelve times (fifteen, if you count the threats of four men). I do not include among these assaults the times I ran like the wind from some stranger who accosted me on an isolated street, in the deserted hall of an office building, or in a quiet corner of a public park.

I find the ambiguity of my claim interesting, for the sexual assaults were sexual insofar as they aimed at certain sexual activities, and they were sexual insofar as I was touched in sexual places in sexual ways. However, I certainly distinguish the assaults which were "attempts" from those assaults which achieved their express purpose. By defeating the actual ends of an attack, I avoided feeling a submission which I by no means felt in the unwanted touches I endured while the battle was still going on. Insofar as the assault remained only an attempt, I was able to avoid the psychological implications of having lost the battle. I was thus able to screen out the actual fact that the attempt itself was already a loss of integrity. From the standpoint of my own psychology it was just as well.

I reacted to the physical sexual assaults the way so many women do. I said nothing. Since I had avoided "rape," I wasn't sure there was anything to say. I told myself to be more wary, more suspicious. I was irritated with myself for having "got myself into it." I became a careful observer of character, of facial expressions. I had delivery men leave things outside the door. I was very careful about walking alone, or about ending up in the same room alone with any man who had not passed all my tests for having a good character. If these were the only consequences of sexual assault, then sexual assault would be serious. But they are not the only consequences.

I said nothing for other reasons. Who would believe that it was really intended, that I wasn't exaggerating, that I hadn't brought it on? And later on, who would believe that it could happen to me so many times? And me not be responsible in some way? When I began to talk about these incidents, I discovered another reason for keeping silent. Few people know how to handle these disclosures. They tended to respond with a silence that made me wonder whether I was believed. I found myself wanting to say "It's not that it's any big deal. . . ." Once I told my story to a psychoanalyst. Predictably, he wondered aloud what I did to cause these attacks.

I wondered too. I began to scrutinize my behavior. Perhaps I was sexy? But the truth is, I didn't really see how. I should not, according to all the fashion magazines, have been the object of overwhelming sexual desire. Maybe I was just one of those women Carl Jung talked about, the sort that fit anima projections? I had not yet heard the theory that rape is motivated more by anger or the desire for power than by sexual desire. My more recent theory of my own is that if I am attacked more than other women it is because I am so often oblivious to the very male who attacks me. To the extent that I tend to be independent and self-absorbed, I may very well anger males who want to be noticed. This would explain why I was so often surprised by my assailants. They tended to belong to the class of men who never really crossed my mind. But then, what if I am not attacked more often than other women?

We don't know how widespread sexual assault is. My suspicion is that if it happened to me it happens to other women like me, especially women in the sort of environment I grew up in. If it does, I doubt they would say anything. They are women who don't have much of a voice; they don't write articles and books; they probably aren't even surveyed that often. And if they were surveyed, I'm not at all convinced they'd talk.

To the extent that I am not typical, it is easy to see how very easily a woman can be raped. Nor are obvious defenses always available to women. A friend of mine who was raped (and not just sexually assaulted) when she was sixteen, told me that she could have reached for her knitting needle, at a crucial moment, and put it through her assailant's eye. She said she just couldn't do it, and preferred being raped to making someone blind. I do not think I would have refrained. (But this does raise the question of what would count as self-defense under these circumstances.)

While the sexual assaults I experienced served the purpose of general intimidation and forced me to the realization that I must maintain a higher state of alertness and caution, I was actually quite proud of myself for preventing the actual rapes. I developed a tough attitude, which I confess I still hold. "When you live in the jungle you have to watch out for the wild animals." But this tough attitude masked an extreme vulnerability concerning my sexual integrity. I would have been totally devastated, unbearably humiliated, had any of the rapes succeeded. I am sure I would have needed serious psychiatric care. It is this very incapacity for enduring such humiliation that made it necessary for me to threaten my assailants with murderous intent.

I'm not sure I am psychologically strong enough to endure a rape, even now, even though I am older, more cynical, more resigned to the evils of the world, more able to distance myself. The younger version of myself could not have. Whether reasonably or not, I took my sexual integrity as seriously as if it were the source of life itself. I have never been a sexual puritan. I have had a rewarding sexual life with lovers, and husbands. Indeed, I think sexual love is just about the loveliest thing in the world. And I certainly feel protective of that loveliness. But there is a deeper reason for my strength of commitment to my sexual integrity. I feel the need to have some power over my life. Growing up in a violent world does not allow a lot of scope for the satisfaction of that need. In my young life I felt very much at the mercy of others. Most of what I could do was dependent on what they decided and what resources they would agree to provide. I was unable to protect myself from quite regular physical violence, and that exacerbated my realization that I did not have control. I learned early that I had limited power over learning, that I was very much at the mercy of bad teachers and poor libraries, and that learning cost money I didn't have. So I could only barely compensate through the exercise of my intellectual prowess. I cathected my need for control onto the socially sanctioned value of sexual integrity. Here I made my last stand. Here I could not be touched. To the degree that I felt powerless everywhere else, I felt Promethean in my defense of my sexual self. It does not matter that I did not really have power. I felt I had power, and I believed this power to be well grounded in absolute right. Thus, my sexual integrity stood as a powerful symbol of my very being, a being that was located, and had to be located, beyond intrusion. There was only one holdout where I exercised my imagined power, and so in the course of events demonstrated the actual power of the imagination.

Actual rape would have devastated me. It would have destroyed a power which was, symbolically, of the highest importance to me, which was, moreover, the only power I really believed I had. I think it is perfectly understandable that people cannot easily tolerate that degree of devastation. In fighting off my would-be rapists, in upholding the symbolism of my sexual integrity, I confirmed my belief in that power. I kept some part of me pure, aloof, pristine, at my own disposal absolutely, for my own particular purposes. I wonder how many women feel this way? I wonder how many men cannot tolerate this presumption of power in women? I wonder to what extent that presumption accounts for the feminist insight that rape is not motivated by desire for sex but by a desire to humiliate. To the extent that it does, it also accounts for the devastation which forced sex so often inflicts. It damages the core of personal integrity in irreparable ways. Such damage cannot be sustained. Perhaps this explains why, when the heroine of Isabel Allende's *House of Spirits* is repeatedly raped by the Chilean police, she is able to find good in that evil. For in forgiving the police and looking forward to the child she is bearing, she takes upon herself a new power, the power of a goddess. She arrogates to herself the power to be merciful, to forgive, and to create good out of evil. The destruction of power implicit in rape is unsustainable. Therefore it must be replaced with a new power, a more powerful power, a goddess's power. But not everyone can effect this displacement.

From my experiences I draw the following conclusions. (1) If evidence of resistance is necessary to establish nonconsent, then women are lost. In the face of considerable force, resistance is simply out of the question. (2) I was very lucky. It is simply amazing that my anger prevailed. Anyone who was less angry or more fearful would simply have been raped. So we must not assume that if I was able to fight off rapists, every woman is. (3) We should not be surprised if women are fiercely attached to their sexual integrity. Most women in this society are not very powerful, and sexual integrity is one thing to which they are allegedly entitled. Accordingly, we should expect women to be quite devastated when it is violated.

We do know, of course, that there are women who feel more powerless than I did, who feel no right to power over anything. We cannot expect them to put their life on the line for their sexual integrity, or even to put up much of a fight, or even, in every case, to go so far as to say "no" in some hesitant "please don't" way. The law, Wells and others have suggested, must protect these women too. I agree. I believe that laws which claim that there is no consent unless there is a "positive response" go some way toward providing that protection.

6

A Dialogue on Evidence

Angela P. Harris and Lois Pineau

Lois: I'm interested in the questions of what evidence is admissible and how it is likely to count, in part because I fear there may be methodological obstacles to discovering when communicative sexuality has occurred.

My first question is about the Fifth Amendment. I take it that the Fifth Amendment gives defendants the right to keep silent. Would this right be likely to work in a defendant's interest? It wouldn't seem so, if the only story before the court was the story of the complainant. Also, what is the extent of this right to keep silent? Can the defendant be selective, answering some question but not others? Or if he agrees to speak, must he speak about everything? I wonder if there is any analogue to this right in common law?

Angela: The Fifth Amendment privilege against self-incrimination gives the defendant the right not to take the stand and testify. Once he decides to testify, though, he must testify fully and be subject to cross-examination on the substance of what he says. So the defendant can't decide to answer some questions and not others, and everything concerning the crime at issue is fair game.

In rape cases, the defendant is probably going to want to testify for the reason you suggest, otherwise it will be just the complainant's story the jury gets to hear. So the Fifth Amendment privilege against self-incrimination doesn't play a big role in rape trials.

Our Fifth Amendment privilege is an extension of English common law. Prior to the mid-seventeenth century, ecclesiastical courts were able to compel self-incriminating testimony from an accused, and this practice was picked up by the Court of the Star Chamber for its political trials. After a number of controversial cases and some action by Parliament, the common law courts began to accept the proposition that it was improper to compel a defendant in a criminal trial, or a witness, to incriminate himself.

Lois: When juries are weighing evidence, are they bound by any kinds of rules? I'm particularly interested in the way juries handle contradictions. For example, if A's story contradicts B's, and A seems more sincere than B, would that count against B's story?

Angela: American criminal law makes a sharp distinction between "questions of law" and "questions of fact," so the judge gives the jury extensive and detailed instructions about what verdict(s) they may issue, what standard they must apply (in a criminal case, the state must always prove the defendant's guilt "beyond a reasonable doubt"), and what evidence they must ignore (if one side successfully objects to evidence the other side has already introduced to the jury). Sometimes, the jury is even told: "You may consider this piece of evidence for this purpose and not another."

But your question seems to be about credibility—How may a jury decide who's telling the truth when there are contradictory stories, how may a jury decide who's more sincere? The answer is, however it wants. These questions are termed "questions of fact," and they are considered issues of common sense on which the jury is the expert, not the judge. So the jury is free to decide A is lying, or B is more sincere, or A's story is full of holes, without any interference (or guidance) from the judge.

Lois: I guess I'm worried that there may be some reason, in principle, why the lack of evidence so common to acquaintance rape tends to lead to acquittal. Suppose all that the jury has is two contradictory stories, and absolutely no evidence to help them decide between the two stories except that one person seems more believable. What would a judge instruct such a jury?

ANGELA: If there is no evidence in the case except for two contradictory stories, then it's likely that the jury will be reminded of its duty to convict only on evidence that proves the crime beyond a reasonable doubt, and that when so reminded it will acquit the defendant.

LOIS: Of course it is necessary to prove the "crime" beyond a reasonable doubt only because it is a crime. If it were a misdemeanor, that level of proof wouldn't be necessary. Am I right about that?

ANGELA: No. Crimes are divided into two classes: "felonies" and "misdemeanors." The primary difference between a felony and a misdemeanor is the kind of punishment that one receives for committing it. So you might spend a little time in jail or have to pay a fine for a misdemeanor, whereas you'd have to go to state prison for a year or more for committing a felony. But the rules of criminal law and evidence that apply are generally the same. The state must prove the defendant guilty beyond a reasonable doubt.

You may be thinking about an "infraction," which is what happens when a police officer writes you a ticket. You can go to court and protest it if you want, but you won't get a full criminal trial, and there's no "beyond a reasonable doubt" standard. But surely we don't want to see police officers writing out tickets for acquaintance rape!

LOIS: Now, the use of "force," it seems to me, functions in sexual assault cases as evidence that the plaintiff is telling the truth.

ANGELA: You are quite right to point out that the value of the resistance requirement, or a "force" requirement, is to generate physical evidence that will corroborate A's story. The notorious fondness of police and prosecutors for complainants who have been seriously beaten and injured stems from this concern. If there is really nothing in the case to suggest a rape occurred except for A's story, the presumption of innocence will probably require acquittal.

By the way, I ought to point out that use of the word "plaintiff" to describe the victim in a criminal case is incorrect. A plaintiff is somebody who brings a lawsuit against somebody else. In a criminal case, the "plaintiff" is the state. The person who was raped is the "complainant."

This may sound like just semantics, but in fact it illustrates something important about a criminal case: the defendant and the complainant are not direct adversaries. It is the state against the defendant. This is why the standard of proof is so high: the state has a built-in advantage against a criminal defendant. The state has more resources, it has the power to lock the defendant up forever or maybe even kill him, and it (usually) has the trust of the jury. So a rape trial isn't technically "his word against hers," although it plays out that way. It is really "his word against the state's."

LOIS: If evidence of force were always required, most nonaggravated sexual assaults could not be proved. Indeed, it would be impossible to prove guilt in many cases of aggravated sexual assault. Suppose, for example, a man raped a woman at gunpoint but denied he did. Isn't it true, though, that other kinds of evidence may establish guilt? Suppose, for example, that the defendant had been overheard boasting prior to the alleged attack that he intended to teach the complainant a lesson. Or suppose he entered her house uninvited, or that the court were convinced that the complainant had always harbored a deep resentment against the defendant.

ANGELA: Of course there are lots of other kinds of corroborating evidence besides cuts and bruises, and this is one reason why proof of "force" (or proof of "resistance," which amounts to the same thing) is no longer a requirement in rape cases. Feminist critics have quite persuasively argued that one important reason for the old "force-resistance" requirement was the assumption that "good" women would rather die than give up their virtue, and therefore anyone who wasn't rather badly beaten up was probably not a "good" woman but a "bad" one who most likely deserved what she got.

But the issues you have raised in your critique challenge us to examine whether we are still harboring similar kinds of assumptions and expectations about how men and women go about having sex, and whether those assumptions and expectations are fair or unfair. When we don't have cuts and bruises, but rather two different stories, what assumptions and expectations will the jury bring into the courtroom with them in order to evaluate the stories they hear?

LOIS: Stories may conflict in two different ways. They may conflict with respect to what the facts of the matter are, and they may conflict with respect to the interpretation of those facts. Thus, if we find ten dollars in one person's pocket, that is a fact concerning which there is little room for differences in interpretation. However, in deciding whether that ten dollars belongs to her, was given to her, or was stolen by her, we must place an interpretation on the way that fact is situated within a larger context. Our predispositions concerning what we regard as expected, or normal, may heavily influence us to choose one interpretation rather than another as more probable.

Consider the following example: Suppose A claims that a recent acquaintance, B, robbed her. Suppose B is indeed possessed of the sum of money A claims to have lost. Suppose furthermore that B admits he got the money from A. How do we know A didn't give B the money and then charge B with theft in order to take some sort of dark revenge on him? We might speculate that A suffered briefly from strong impulses of generosity, impulses that she later regretted acting upon. We might hypothesize that the woman had been hoping to buy friendship, and that she took her revenge when she realized she had been betrayed.

Now, it is clear that if we were at all inclined to believe in the frequency of such behavior, few thieves would ever be convicted. If we even thought such behavior occurred occasionally, many more thieves would be given the benefit of the doubt. The point here is not to draw an analogy between date rape and robbery, but rather to illustrate the extent to which our predispositions to believe some things influence our interpretations of other things. It enables us to see how a shift in expectations regarding normal behavior would make a difference with respect to what we are willing to interpret as consent. If we suppose that it is normal for a woman's struggles to convey agreement and for her "no" to mean yes, then precious few struggles will ever be interpreted as assaults. If, however, we suppose it is normal for prospective lovers to be attentive and considerate, if we presume that under conditions of seduction there is a heightened-care requirement, then most struggles and refusals *will* be interpreted as assaults.

If it is to be effective, a change in law which invokes communicative sexuality as a paradigm requires that judges and jurors accept the paradigm. So part of the struggle to win justice would have to take place at the level of jury selection. Is it absolutely impossible to select a jury that will accept communicative sex as a paradigm?

ANGELA: The prosecution will of course try to select jurors who are open to the idea of communicative sexuality as a norm, but the defense will be looking for more hidebound people. In most jurisdictions, both sides get a number of "peremptory" challenges, meaning that no reason need be given for rejecting that juror. The theory behind this is that the jury that results from this adversarial process will be fair to both sides. In practice, it is very difficult to predict in advance how the jury dynamics will operate.

LOIS: If the law clearly stated that women have a right to communicative sexuality, could a prospective juror who was opposed to that right be selected?[1] Can a prospective juror be asked whether she thinks women have such a right? Suppose a prospective juror thinks that women should not have that right. Could she still, in principle, serve on a jury at a trial aimed at determining whether that right had been violated?

ANGELA: I suppose I don't know where that "right" would come from, or how it would work. Of course, a state legislature could pass a statute saying that a woman has a "right" to communicative sexuality, and the statute could define what that means. I see three kinds of problems with this approach. The biggest is getting such a statute passed—it would be a very controversial battle! Usually rights (except those in the U.S. Constitution) are more concrete and behavior-oriented than this. Would this new "right" mean that people who are bad lovers can be sued by their female partners for thousands of dollars? What about men—don't they have a right to communicative sexuality too? If you have a "right" to communicative sexuality, does this mean the state has to provide you with it if you aren't getting any? Isn't this just another example of Americans trying to impose New Age, "politically correct," touchy-feely, therapeutic values on everybody, or trying to ruin love and affection by making it a legal issue? And so on.

1. On recent legislation in Canada, see the beginning of Chapter 5 in this book.

Second, even if such a statute were passed, and was said to apply only in criminal cases, there is the question of how it would interact with the rape statute. Perhaps it would be a rule of evidence, where the judge would tell the jury what they should take as the standard of ordinary sexuality. This, I think, is what you are looking for. But the defense would argue that this doesn't change the standard of proof in a criminal case, or change what the prosecution must prove under the rape statute. So there would be many legal battles over how to harmonize your new "right" with the preexisting rape statute.

Finally, there is the question of getting the jury to understand what "communicative sexuality" means and to apply the new standard correctly. The defense, of course, will try to interpret it in the narrowest possible way. In the end, it will still be his word against hers.

LOIS: What about jury instruction? Isn't it the duty of the judge to inform the jury about what the law is, and in so doing also to inform the jury about the intent of the lawmakers? In other words, if the law were very clear on what communicative sex is, if it laid it down that "no" means no, wouldn't the jury be expected to apply the law?

ANGELA: It is true that the judge must instruct the jury on what the law is, and so jury instructions provide one opportunity for education. The problems here are practical. First, it isn't clear how well juries are able really to understand jury instructions (which are often in "legalese") and how well they are able to follow the instructions assuming they do understand them. Second, there is no check on whether the jury correctly applies the law. The jury's verdict is simply "guilty" or "not guilty," so in practice there is a lot of room for the jurors to filter the facts and the law through their own prejudices.

LOIS: From what you and others have said, I infer that a jury is a kind of "black box" in which process is suspended. As we have seen in the Rodney King and O. J. Simpson verdicts, there are no checks on whether a jury decides a matter rationally or irrationally, in a fair manner or in a prejudiced manner. This makes me even less certain that it is reasonable to deal with the widespread problem of date rape at the level of *criminal* law. As you know, I have suggested that the problem of nonaggravated sexual assault might be better handled by reducing it to a misdemeanor.

ANGELA: As a student of criminal law, my problem with your solution is that the culpability requirement (that is, requiring some form of *mens rea*) is an important principle in criminal law. Strict liability crimes tend to be regulatory offenses rather than serious felonies. I have problems with the notion of putting someone in prison and giving them a very serious criminal record without any proof of a guilty mind.

LOIS: Yes, but of course if nonaggravated sexual assault were a misdemeanor, then convicted persons precisely would not acquire a serious criminal record. So the objection cannot be that the crime is too serious to warrant eliminating *mens rea,* but rather that it is necessary to maintain its seriousness.

The most obvious reasons in support of my suggestion have to do with strategy. With a misdemeanor, it is possible to require "strict liability." This means that if it is established that a person violated the law, he may be guilty whether he meant to do so or not. This clearly dispenses with the need to establish *mens rea,* "a guilty mind." Since rape convictions often fail because *mens rea* is defeated, and since *mens rea* may be defeated in many jurisdictions on the basis of a man's "honest belief" in a woman's consent, and since "honest belief" is all too easy a defense in the present ideological environment, elimination of the *mens rea* is an obvious and effective strategy.

My second reason for suggesting that nonaggravated sexual assault be a misdemeanor is precisely that misdemeanor offenses are less serious. The strategy I have in mind is that by reducing the seriousness of nonaggravated sexual assault we might be able to obtain a higher conviction rate. My hypothesis is that a higher conviction rate would actually provide more protection for women, and that the increased probability of getting a conviction would lead more women to report sexual assaults and to prosecute their assailants.

A third reason is a more general concern about the wisdom of taking punitive approaches to solving social problems. Sexual assault is a lot like woman-battering. There is a certain banality to the evil, an everydayness about it that draws attention to the dark and ugly shadow side of persons who are not entirely moral monsters. Men batter their wives and girlfriends when they can get away with it. In many cases, effective intervention by the courts, combined with education and therapy, puts a stop to it without incarcerating the guilty men. There are many reasons for the non-aggravated kinds of sexual assault. Overall, I think such assaults issue from the extreme emphasis on satisfying macho requirements. Sometimes these requirements are met in a ruthless and calculating way. Other times they are part of a general confusion and ignorance about how to act. I suspect that this misled masculinity can be corrected without applying extreme sanctions. On this point, I am tempted to see date rape as more analogous to dangerous driving than to murder. Both are potentially traumatic and socially intolerable. Like date rape, dangerous driving can be linked to the satisfaction of macho requirements. Yet it is possible to think of dangerous driving as something that is easily checked, on the one hand, by relatively light sanctions that are nonetheless difficult and expensive to avoid and, on the other hand, by educational programs that teach us the pointlessness of foolish and reckless driving.

In order for my suggestion to be acceptable, it is necessary to disrupt the connection between sexual assault and the extreme seriousness that is attached to it, a seriousness that finds expression in strong punitive reactions. It is important to be clear on exactly where the seriousness of sexual assault does lie, and so to ensure that our remedies for it are not archaic. It is helpful to understand the source of these reactions.

In almost every culture that values the sexual purity and fidelity of women, sexual assault is not only an assault. It has, traditionally, devalued the woman raped, usually to the point of ruining her future. A virgin would lose her chance to marry, and her family would lose her bride-price. In many cultures, a married woman might be divorced, and thus lose her only vocation. Of course, this devaluation could not happen to women who were already disreputable, which explains why, for so long, rape was a crime only against "respectable" women. It is clear that, throughout most of history, underclass women were raped more or less with impunity, though of course it could not be called rape because there were no laws restricting sexual access. The extension of protection to women "sans repute" is a quite recent phenomenon.

There is a big difference between an assault which ruins a woman's only chance to live a decent life and one which has only a small effect upon her social and economic future. In order to make rape the horrendous crime it was in the past, it is necessary to invest its psychological effects and health risks with all the import contained in its former social and economic effects.

There is no question that rape may have serious psychological effects. Even nonaggravated sexual assault—assault which, arguably, did not involve injury, torture, or threat of death—nonetheless takes place within a cultural system of symbols and meanings which causes intense shame, anger, and humiliation. It also functions as the worst sort of insult, expressing to the victim utter contempt for her autonomy, and hence for her worth as a person. Occasionally, however, it will not express anything so strong, but rather constitute the milder sort of insult involved when two wills cross and, for the moment, one person rides roughshod over the other. In light of the risk to health that date rape so often presents to women, however, I believe that the milder sort of case would be a rare occurrence.

Sexual assault involving penetration always puts the assaulted party at risk. Unwanted sex, in addition to being unwanted, always brings with it the risk of pregnancy, venereal disease, and, these days, even death. It thus places a woman's health at serious risk, and in this respect alone is probably more threatening than reckless driving. However, one hardly ever reads of the dangers implied by the epidemic of sexual assaults to which women are victim. The enormity of women's oppression thus continues to be hidden behind a system of justice which both acquits their assailants and at the same time refuses to acknowledge the irrationality which is involved in engaging in any sex which is not "safe sex," though it is unlikely that sexual assault will ever be safe.

It is important to develop strategies that will bring about a higher conviction rate, in part because such conviction rates might enable women to avoid the great risk to health that they incur under the present circumstances. For we must not lose track of the fact that there is at present no redress for most women for most rapes. And this state of affairs, it seems to me, is an intolerable one. It is far more important to remedy this situation than it is to avoid convicting some aggressive dolt of a misdemeanor just because he was too clued out to know that he should treat resistance as a form of denial.

It is clear, as well, that the principle of respect for persons would be better satisfied by raising the conviction rate for sexual crimes. Women whose autonomy has been denied are entitled, even where the effects of that denial are little more than the insult suffered, to strong social recognition of the importance of that autonomy. Such recognition, it seems to me, shores up one's sense of dignity and makes the insult easier to bear. I fear that as long as nonaggravated sexual assault is a serious felony, the result will be, on the one hand, a kind of overkill and, on the other hand, a continued undermining of the very sense of dignity which is most in need of being restored. The reasons for this are well known. First, the setup is one in which the victim is, because of the seriousness with which crime is regarded, put on trial. Second, the standards of proof are so high that her assailant is frequently acquitted, leaving her with no social recognition at all of the indignity she has suffered. Thus, instead of indignity being redressed, indignity is added to indignity. Moreover, we must come up with a solution. Decriminalization, with its less severe penalties and lower standards of proof, seems to be an obvious logical solution.

ANGELA: One favorite law professor hypothetical is the woman who makes a habit of seducing traveling salesmen and then one day is surprised by her husband coming home early and says she has been raped. I suspect that such situations are the product of male imagination.

LOIS: Yes, and almost every man I have ever talked to on this issue imagines that if women could get away with it they would seek revenge on men by accusing them of rape. I am led to suspect that a belief in feminine revenge dominates the masculine imagination. It is fascinating to speculate on the reason. The expectation does seem to suggest a guilty mind. I can think, off hand, of two sources. The first is that the great masculine social unconscious is aware of the injustice women must feel over their second-sex status and attributes to them a corresponding motive for revenge. The second is a deep sense of guilt over any imagined "sexual imposition." Again, the reaction to unconscious, or maybe not so unconscious, guilt may be to attribute punitive reactions to women.

ANGELA: I do appreciate your reasons for wanting both to obtain more convictions and to make nonaggravated sexual assault a lesser crime. And I do think men harbor a deep-seated uneasiness, if not guilt, about "what women really want," which is played out in public policy. But I think you are trying to have it both ways. As we have seen in the past few years with recent high-profile criminal cases, there are two courts: the court of law and the court of public opinion. Criminal law has to maintain some kind of relationship with people's ordinary moral sense, or else people will be incensed and petition their political representatives to change the law.

Making nonaggravated sexual assault a strict liability crime means, in effect, that even if it would be completely impossible and unreasonable for the man to believe that the woman was engaging in the sexual act against her will (or, perhaps, that she thought the sex was insufficiently "communicative"), he would still be convicted. Yes, it would be only a misdemeanor, not a felony, so he wouldn't be required to report it on subsequent job applications and such. But a crime is a crime, and I think most people think of crimes—especially sexual ones—as deeply immoral. Strict liability works because its targets are usually corporations, whose "intent" is fictive anyway. But strict liability crimes for people have long been controversial for this very reason—crime and moral blameworthiness go together. If you are going to convict a person of a crime, then you are morally stigmatizing him, and so the state should at least have to show he acted unreasonably or recklessly. If you are going to say "But this isn't really a serious crime," then why should it be a crime at all? And how will it bolster the autonomy of women to see their boyfriends given a slap on the wrist and sent back to them newly bitter?

I suspect your conviction rate would not increase as much as you might expect, because there would be resistance to the implementation of a strict liability rule. Prosecutors would hesitate to charge, and juries would hesitate to convict. Moreover, the political backlash might well fall most heavily on the young women you are trying to "protect." The media story would be about whining or vengeful young women who get their inexperienced lovers convicted of crimes.

I do see your point that making rape a terrible crime and punishing it harshly can be a strategy of hypocrisy. No one really gets punished because it's such a terrible crime, and everyone gets to feel morally sanctimonious. But I think your point about "the wisdom of taking punitive approaches to solving social problems" actually cuts against you here. I share your view that date rape is more like dangerous driving than like murder. But does the way to get more people to feel that way really lie in changing the criminal law—an extremely blunt instrument at best? Perhaps we ought to make date rape a relatively minor offense, but I am not sure that in itself will have the educative benefits we would both like to see.

LOIS: It has always seemed to me a piece of modern barbarism that a woman's past sexual history should be thought to have any relevance to her present complaint. It is absurd to suppose that a prostitute can't be raped, but that is precisely the sort of assumption underlying this very persistent idea that promiscuity undermines credibility. My understanding, however, is that the sexual history of the complainant is no longer considered to have much bearing on her motive for making an unsubstantiated accusation.

ANGELA: You are right about that. Under the Federal Rules of Evidence and in most states, "rape shield" laws are in place. There are several types of rape shield statutes, but all preclude the admission of the complainant's past sexual history to show that because she consented before she probably did this time as well. Prior sexual conduct is also now inadmissible to impeach the victim's credibility—that is, to show she is a "dishonest woman." Prior sexual conduct remains admissible to show a modus operandi, but those cases are few and far between.

There are loopholes in the rape shield laws. Under the federal rape shield law, prior sexual conduct is still admissible to show that a person other than the defendant is the source of semen, pregnancy, or injury. Prior sexual conduct with the accused is also still admissible—the reasoning "She consented before, so she probably did so again" is considered valid. What do you think about this exception, as a logician?

LOIS: The reasoning, allegedly from induction, is that if a woman consented to have sex with an acquaintance in the past she probably did so this time, prior to charging him with sexual assault. But this is a good inductive argument only if it supports the relevant connection—namely, that in the past a pattern has been established according to which as a general rule consensual relations with a partner are followed by accusing that partner of sexual assault.

Suppose:

"P" stands for "A consents to having sex with B,"

and

"Q" stands for "A would charge B with sexual assault."

What we need in order to ground the conclusion that a woman would both consent to have sex with someone and then charge him with sexual assault is to establish that a pattern exists represented by the general rule "If P, then Q"—i.e., if A consented to have sex with B, then A would charge B with sexual assault." The prospect of discovering such a pattern, however, seems highly implausible.

On the other hand, if we assume that consensual relations between a woman and a man are not usually followed by her accusing him of sexual assault, induction will actually support a conclusion contrary to the one the courts used to draw, for the inductive evidence will confer more probability on the conclusion that if she had consented to sex she would not have filed a complaint. We may formalize the argument as follows.

Suppose the pattern established is "If P, then not-Q"—i.e., "If A consented to have sex with B, then A would not charge B with sexual assault." Then by *modus tollens,* if "not-Q" is negated—i.e., "A does charge B with sexual assault," it follows that "not-P," i.e., "A did not consent to having sex with B."[2]

ANGELA: Finally, because constitutional rights override statutory rights, evidence of a woman's prior sexual history is still admissible whenever the defendant's constitutional rights to a fair trial would be jeopardized by its exclusion. But this is a matter for the trial judge to decide in a particular case—which still leaves room for your aggression-acquiescence model of sexuality to color the judge's decision about when evidence is relevant.

In other words, suppose we have a complainant who has been working as a prostitute and then says she has been raped by a new customer. Under the rape shield laws, the mere fact that she has had sex consensually in the past does not mean that she therefore did this time too. But suppose the defendant argues passionately

2. *Modus tollens* is the rule. If "If X then Y," then if "not-Y" then "not-X."

that not being able to introduce the complainant's history as a prostitute destroys his right to a fair trial, and the judge agrees. Then, in the name of upholding constitutional rights, the judge can disregard the rape shield statute and allow the jury to consider the complainant's background as relevant to the case. This would be an example of the judge's firm belief in the aggression-acquiescence model of sexuality being given the force of constitutional law.

Such cases, however, are likely to be very rare, for the trial judge would have to present a better reason for not enforcing the rape shield law than "I don't think the rape shield law is fair." The judge would have to explain why this case was uniquely unfair to this particular defendant.

But here's an issue that really does arise.

One of the hot issues in evidence law today has to do not with consent as a defense but with the defendant's argument that even though she didn't actually consent he thought that she did. This is the "reasonable mistake" rule. Under the rape shield statutes, the question is whether the defendant is still free to introduce evidence of the complainant's past sexual history, not to prove actual consent but to prove his own mental state of mistake as to consent. There is one federal case (*Doe v. United States*, 666 F.2d 43, 4th Cir. 1981) that says that he can. This punches a hole in the rape shield laws, for the ulterior motive of introducing evidence of the complainant's past sexual life is to trade on deeply rooted beliefs that loose women ask for it or can't be raped, and even if the jury is told to use the evidence to decide not actual consent but mistake about consent, this evidence will probably have the desired effect.

Lois: Yes, I'm aware of this move. This is the "honest belief" defense, and as I mentioned in my original article it is precisely the defense I am arguing against. As long as it works as a defense, we will go around in the same old circles, and women will receive no more protection from the law in the future than they have in the past. It is to counter this offense that I think we need to develop a criterion of "a reasonable belief" and to drop the *mens rea* requirement. A criterion of reasonable belief is needed not to establish *mens rea* but rather to establish the conditions under which judges and juries may come to decide if a felony has occurred.

Angela: Another hot issue in rape evidence law is whether evidence of "rape trauma syndrome" should be admissible, and for what purpose. This evidence usually takes the form of a psychiatric social worker or other expert who testifies about characteristic behavior patterns of people who have been raped (e.g., insomnia, fear of being alone, repeatedly reliving the event). One issue is whether such testimony meets the test for admissible expert testimony (is this science or just quackery?). A second issue is, if "rape trauma syndrome" is sufficiently recognized by the relevant scientific community, to what uses can this testimony be put? Can it be introduced to prove that the complainant was actually raped? Or can it be introduced only to correct the jury's misconceptions about how people who have been raped ought to behave? The answer seems to be no to the first question and yes to the second.

Both the rape shield laws and rape trauma syndrome evidence are ways of correcting misconceptions jurors might have about the way the world works. Both these endeavors have been met with suspicion because the usual tendency in American law is to treat the jury as a black box and assume that whatever decision it makes must represent the best that common sense can come up with.

Lois: We are becoming increasingly aware that "common sense" varies, depending on which end of the stick we are on. What is common sense to me, who wants protection from rape, will not be common sense to men who want to maintain immunity from prosecution for rape. The problem, I take it, is not whether rape trauma occurs but whether it is always possible to know that it has occurred in a particular case.

The fact that it does occur is shown very well by the story of the Scarborough rapist, a serial rapist who follows women from their bus stops late at night and who is quite violent and given to choking his victims. The Metro Toronto police have samples of his blood, hair, skin, and semen, so they know with certainty when it is he who has attacked a woman. One such woman was found late at night, between her bus stop and her home in a disoriented condition with bruises on her neck. A medical examination proved that she had been raped by the Scarborough rapist. However, the woman had no memory of the event.[3]

Of course, the evidence is seldom so compelling. The fear will

3. The Scarborough rapist is Paul Bernardo, who has recently confessed and is now serving time as a dangerous offender.

always be that the woman is prevaricating or exaggerating or obsessed in some way. This is the problem of "inner states." The relationship between inner states and evidence for them is one of the most intractable in philosophy, extremely interesting, and worth looking into on its own. There must be a body of law on this issue already. After all, people make insurance claims based on pain and suffering, and pain and suffering are inner states. I wonder what kind of presumptions operate in those cases?

ANGELA: As you might have already guessed from my comments, the law deals with the problem of inner states in two ways. First, the problem is sometimes given to the jury with no guidance at all. The theory there is that in ordinary life we attribute inner states to people all the time, using our "common sense," and that's what we ask the jury to do. Second, the jury is sometimes given the guidance of "expert testimony," and here the problem becomes telling the real experts from the fakes. A real expert is somebody who can bolster (or correct) common sense with ways of knowing that derive from science. The underlying controversy over the rape trauma expert is whether "rape trauma" has met the standards of the scientific community or whether it is just the product of people seeking expert-witness fees.

The question you raise about pain and suffering in tort cases is an interesting one, I agree. My understanding is that the jury is left to its own common sense. Often they are shown "a day in the life" videos of the plaintiff going about her daily activities in obvious pain, or testimony is introduced about the amount and number of pain medications the plaintiff is taking. But essentially the jury is asked to use its imagination to reconstruct another person's inner state, and then put a dollar value on it—the most peculiar operation of all!

LOIS: Is it clear that if rape trauma syndrome can be established it ought to *count* as evidence that a woman was raped? Logically, it would not *establish* that she had been raped, for there could be some other reason for the trauma. In this respect, it would be like bruises, cuts, and swellings. Incurred around the time of the assault, they count as evidence, even though they could in principle have been caused by a recent automobile accident. And I don't see how, logically, anything could count as evidence of a woman's disoriented behavior without at the same time counting as evidence that something rather shocking or violent caused the disoriented behavior.

ANGELA: I agree with you about the import of rape trauma evidence. The real question, as I have suggested, is whether this evidence is flagged for the jury as "scientific" (implying that they ought to believe the expert's word about it) or admitted solely as evidence to be subjected to common sense, meaning that the jurors are left to sort out its significance on their own.

But let's get back to the essential message of your article.

As a feminist, I do applaud your communicative sexuality model as an ethical guide. In fact, your model very much resembles the sexuality of people in the S/M community, who put both psychological dominance and submission and various forms of extreme physical sensation at the core of their sexuality, instead of genital intercourse. The ethic of S/M is that the people who participate in a "scene" must always be in communication about what they are doing. Practices like "safe words" for people on the "bottom" (for example, "yellow" means you need to stop very soon; "red" means stop now) ensure that people can experience very intense emotional and physical sensations in a completely consensual and hence "safe" environment. I am fascinated by how much these "sexual outlaws," often derided or pitied by the majority as "perverts," have created a sexuality that is more feminist than the sexuality of "normal people." I am also fascinated by how this sexuality, like the one you propose as a model, depends on clear communication.

But, like Catharine Wells, I must confess that I am worried about the way in which you propose that communicative sexuality be not just a good idea but the law. If communicative sexuality becomes the law, who gets to determine how much and what kind of communication is enough? There is a problem here of entrusting the interpretation of norms to people who may not understand them and may well be hostile to them—a problem that is also raised by the feminist antipornography campaign. I am suggesting that "communicative sexuality" as the law may end up being quite far from "communicative sexuality" as an ethic.

Another problem is the one of hard cases. There are almost always hard cases when important legal doctrines are at stake, so this is not an argument against your standard. But as the devil's advocate, I want to ask you to clarify your position. Let's go back to the hypothetical case you described in your article, where a woman communicates ambivalence which the man takes for consent. In a world where communicative sexuality really was the norm, such a situation would hardly ever arise. But we live in *this* world. Should such a situation be a crime, even a misdemeanor given very little punishment?

LOIS: Now it is precisely on this point that there seems to be a great deal of opposition, and that surprises me. Perhaps my position is not yet clear.

First, communicative sex, as I conceive of it, is consistent with engaging in every kind of sex. Just as we have always supposed that people may engage in any kind of sex they like so long as it is consensual, we can now say that people may engage in any kind of sex they like so long as it is communicative. Thus, partners may have rough or gentle sex, oral or anal sex, sadomasochistic or voyeuristic sex, as long as they do not take for granted that they know what kind of sex each other wants without bothering to check. And "checking" requires communication, and communication requires the care and listening to the desires of the other without which it is entirely pointless. All I have added to the old notion that all sexual expression should be consensual is the further idea that we consent without exchanging information. I have argued, it is true, that there are certain presumptions about what things mean, and about what a communicative atmosphere requires, that confer more probability on certain interpretations than they do on others. But none of these presumptions rules out any particular kind of sexual practice. This point has been acknowledged by SAMOIS, a lesbian feminist sadomasochist group, in its book *Coming to Power*. The group argues persuasively that they practice sadomasochistic sex with full consensuality, and they maintain that this is possible precisely because they have a well-worked-out system of communication, a system in which screaming and struggling might not mean "stop" but some other signal always does. It seems to me that this kind of signal is clearly a requirement of "rough sex." Without it, it is impossible in principle to draw a distinction between "rough sex" and slavery.

The second point I want to make is that my position is a feminist position. This means that some people, nonfeminists in particular, will not agree to it. When the suffragettes lobbied to get women the vote, they were not able to please all women because not all women wanted to vote. In fact, many women didn't want the vote. I am prepared to accept that just as some women did not want the right to vote, some women did not want the right to communicative sex. However, this is no argument against it. There is no more force to such a position than there is to that of a slave who is opposed to the abolition of slavery.

I think that your concern, and Catharine's concern, is that some feminists might succeed in having their sexual standards held up in a way that discriminates in some way against the sexual pleasures of others. But if the general expectation of communicative interaction is consistent with every particular kind of sexual pleasure, I do not see how this could happen. The only possible pleasure that could be ruled out is the pleasure of rape itself. But surely you don't want to say that we should not have laws against rape because someone, somewhere, may take pleasure in rape?

The third point I want to make is actually twofold. I draw attention to two distinctions. The first is between *accepting a paradigm* and *imposing a paradigm.* If communicative sex is to be taken as a norm, that is not at all the same thing as legislating it. Insofar as we take communicative sex as a norm, we expect it to be the kind of sex that rational, considerate people engage in. In order to *impose* communicative sex, we would have to send spies into the bedrooms of the nation. That is impractical, and even if it were not I would not favor it. If people who have sex which is not communicative do not wish to complain, that is, at one level, their concern. We may, of course, be concerned about the setup in which people develop such desires, but that concern addresses a different though related problem. Probably the best the law can do is provide proper redress for those who do complain. An analogous case can be made for someone who flashes her bankroll in a seedy joint and then wanders home alone down otherwise deserted back alleys. If she is robbed but doesn't register a complaint, there is little the law can do, but if she does register a complaint, the law is obliged to act. However much we might think she set herself up, however much we might decry either her foolishness or her innocence, she has still been robbed, and the thief is guilty.

The analogy illustrates the second distinction I want to draw—

between having a right and enforcing the use of that right. These are, again, quite different things. I have a right to vote, but I am not forced to vote. I have a right to an abortion, but no one would force me to have an abortion. I have a right to my property, but no one forces me to keep it. Analogously, I want to argue that women must have a right to communicative sex. It doesn't follow that they will be forced to have communicative sex. Mind you, a man who has noncommunicative sex with a woman would do so at his peril, just as a man who helped himself to my property would do so at his peril. But on the whole, we think the law is too intrusive when it forces us to prosecute for injuries that we do not actually mind. No one would say, however, that we should therefore not have laws against inflicting injury.

The fourth point I want to make is that *communicative sex is normal sex.* The aggressive-acquiescence model of sexual interaction really is a *myth.* It is, like the romances published by Harlequin, a harmful fantasy served up to confused teenagers, the severely repressed, and the uncommunicative. On account of its history, the myth has come to be bound up in a certain legal conceptual framework. It is precisely what, when foolishly acted on, turns out to be rape. Reasonable persons of goodwill do, habitually, have communicative sex. I feel that my job as a philosopher is simply to remind people of the implications of this.

It is clear from so many of the responses I've had that no one is willing to jeopardize the chance to have rough sex. I'm not completely sure what this term designates, but it is obvious to me that we can distinguish, in principle, between rough sex that is communicative and rough sex that is not. Furthermore, we are very good at precisely this kind of a distinction, and I find it very hard to believe people who deny this.

I shall illustrate what I mean by describing Eros at work in a reggae bar I visited recently. The bar in question was full of young coeds, and I was struck by the degree of rough sexual play in which these young people engaged. In one case, two men had cornered a fashionably slim, lightweight woman. One picked her up by the hips and pushed her into a corner where another was waiting. The second man encircled her from behind, pinning her arms down. I was prepared for a rerun from *The Accused,* for she was clearly helpless and their overtures were decidedly sexual. But the woman was just as clearly pleased by this physical encounter. She laughed flirtatiously and was able to twist around sufficiently to plant an abundant number of kisses on each man's lips. After a good deal of laughing and kissing they let her go. However suspect this description might sound, I was convinced that the woman in question was enjoying the sexual charge she was getting from these energetic and handsome young men, and I was impressed by the guiltless delight she was able to take in her pleasure. Although the scene was rough, she was by no means a passive victim. Had she become angry and resistant, had she screamed or struggled to free herself, it would have been an entirely different encounter, one in which the clear and immediate moral requirement would have been for the young men to let her go.

So the answer to the question "Who gets to decide?" is, necessarily, the same sort of people who have always decided. It is just that now we must ask those same sorts of people to look at things differently and to call on resources which certainly enough people have—the knowledge of language, of body language, and of human nature, which enables us to know all too well when others are angry, frightened, and resisting. I believe that no one has looked for this kind of evidence, for the obvious reason that such evidence did not count. Once we decide that it does count, I suspect the evidence will be found.

Some feminists might object, in the above example, that the woman was indeed submitting to rough tactics and that the only acceptable submission was one which pretended complicity. They might maintain that this woman was so oppressed that she made men's desires her desires, even to the point of responding pleasingly to virtual strangers. That is, indeed, more than a possibility. I have known such women, women so concerned with pleasing that they would be in danger of doing themselves in if it would save a mass murderer the trouble. It is important to understand the forces that colonize women in this way, but the colonized woman's positive overtures must be respected just as much as her negative responses. The way to deal with the problem of colonization is not to doubt the consent of the colonized but to raise with her the question of whether she should indeed consent. It is by engaging her in debate, not by patronizingly denying the legitimacy of her decision, that we both respect her personhood and at the same time stand the best chance of promoting her independence. In other words, the problem of colonization is a different problem and needs to be addressed on a different front.

The crucial point with respect to communicative sex is that, on the communicative model, "no" means no. This is the main practical difference between my view and the old view. On the old view, a woman's prospective lover was entitled to assume that she didn't mean what she said. Now, not only feminists but just about everyone who is concerned with the epidemic problem of rape have thought that no one should be entitled to make this assumption. The right of men to make this assumption certainly must be illegitimate. If we continue to support this right, there is no chance that we can offer women more protection from rape. If we want to challenge this right, I do not see any other way than to change the rules in such a way that a woman's expressed reluctance means just that. This is, we might say, a minimum requirement of communicative sex. To say, therefore, that some people might not like communicative sex, that they might not want a distinction between "rough sex" and slavery, and that therefore a right to communicative sex must not be protected is to allow that a woman's expressed reluctance must not be accepted as a condition of nonconsent. I do not believe that many feminists would want to hold this position. In fact, I think that a difference on this particular point really must delineate the difference between a feminist stance and a nonfeminist stance.

Appendixes:
The Antioch Policy

Appendix 1

The Antioch College
Sexual Offense Policy

[Editor's Note: The Antioch College Sexual Offense Policy was adopted in February 1991 by the Administrative Council (AdCil), which is composed of faculty, students, administrators, and staff. The policy is currently in the process of being revised.

The policy is reprinted here with the permission of Antioch College. It consists of an introduction, titled "Sexual Violence and Safety," and the policy itself.

Antioch College is a small, residential liberal arts college in Ohio; it is now part of Antioch University, which has campuses in a number of urban areas. The policy applies to the College only, not to the other campuses, which are largely nonresidential and serve many nontraditional students.

According to Karen Hall, Director of the Sexual Offense Prevention and Survivors' Advocacy Program at Antioch College, the policy will be reviewed by a task force in the winter of 1996. It is unlikely that there will be changes in the basic goals and structure of the policy, but clarifications are expected. For example, section 2 of the consent policy requires the person initiating sexual conduct to take responsibility for obtaining verbal consent. The section is silent as to responsibility for consent when sexual conduct is mutually initiated. A likely clarification is that responsibility for consent will be mutual when initiation is mutual.]

Sexual Violence and Safety

The statistics on the frequency of sexual violence on college campuses today are alarming. While we try to make Antioch a safe environment for everyone, we still have problems here. There is date and acquaintance rape, and stranger rape, and, while the majority of perpetrators are men and the majority of victims are women, there are also female perpetrators and male victims. There are also many students who have already experienced sexual violence before arriving at Antioch; healing from that experience may be an integral part of their personal, social and academic lives while they are here.

Antioch has a Sexual Offense Prevention and Survivors' Advocacy Program which consists of an Advocate and trained Peer Advocates and Educators. They can talk with you confidentially about any questions or concerns you have, provide or arrange for counseling, and help you access resources about healing from sexual violence. They also provide advocacy for rape victims dealing with a hospital, police, the courts, and/or campus administrative procedures. The program is located on the second floor of Long Hall, next to Maples and above the infirmary. The telephone number is PBX 459 (767-6459). There is also a Rape Crisis Line at PBX 458 (767-6458) which you can call in an emergency. If you experience sexual harassment or assault on co-op, you can call us for support through 1-800-841-1314.

Antioch has two policies, a sexual harassment policy and a sexual offense policy, which have been designed to help deal with these problems when they occur on campus and/or when they involve an Antioch community member. Read these policies; you are held responsible for knowing them. Under the sexual offense policy:

- All sexual contact and conduct between any two people must be consensual;
- Consent must be obtained verbally before there is any sexual contact or conduct;
- If the level of sexual intimacy increases during an interaction (i.e., if two people move from kissing while fully clothed—which is one level—to undressing for direct physical contact, which is another level), the people involved need to express their clear verbal consent before moving to that new level;
- If one person wants to *initiate* moving to a higher level of sexual intimacy in an interaction, *that person is responsible for getting the verbal consent of the other person(s) involved before moving to that level;*
- If you have had a particular level of sexual intimacy before with someone, you must still ask each and every time;
- If you have a sexually transmitted disease, you must disclose it to a potential sexual partner.

Don't ever make any assumptions about consent: they can hurt someone and get you in trouble. Also, do not take silence as consent; it isn't. Consent must be clear and verbal (i.e., saying: yes, I want to kiss you also).

Special precautions are necessary if you, or the person with whom you would like to be sexual, are under the influence of alcohol, drugs, or prescribed medication. Extreme caution should always be used. Consent, even verbal consent, may not be meaningful. Taking advantage of someone who is "under the influence" is never acceptable behavior. If, for instance, you supply someone with alcohol and get her/him drunk so that person will consent to have sex with you (figuring you wouldn't get "as far" if that person were sober), then their consent may be meaningless and you may be charged under the sexual offense policy. If you are so drunk that you act with someone totally inappropriately (in a way maybe you wouldn't if you were sober), or if you are so drunk you don't hear "no," you may still be charged under the sexual offense policy.

If you have a hard time knowing or setting your own personal boundaries, or respecting other people's boundaries, you may have a harder time if alcohol or drugs are involved. For truly consensual sex, you and your partner(s) should be sober to be sexual.

Sexual harassment should be reported to the Advocate; depending on the wishes of the complainant, mediation may be attempted or the charge may be referred to the Hearing Board. Other forms of sexual offenses are also reported to the Advocate, and depending on the wishes of the victim/survivor may be referred for mediation or to the Hearing Board which hears cases of sexual offenses where the alleged offender is a student. If the accused violator is not a student, the case may be referred for follow-up to the appropriate person. In cases of rape and sexual assault, reporting to law enforcement authorities is also encouraged. Anonymous reports may also be made. Complaint forms are in a box outside the program offices in Long Hall, or you can make a report directly to the Advocate, either in person or at PBX 459. All reports are treated confidentially; every attempt is made to treat everyone involved fairly, and to honor the wishes of the victim regarding what is done (or not done).

If you are raped or sexually assaulted:
- Get somewhere safe.
- Contact a friend you trust, a hall advisor, or HAC and/or
- Contact a peer advocate or the Advocate directly, or through the Rape Crisis Line at PBX 458.
- You may also wish to notify the police.
- Do not bathe, change clothes, or otherwise clean-up yet.

The peer advocate or Advocate will provide emotional support, help you to understand your thoughts and feelings at the time, explain your options to you, and support you in whatever decisions you choose to make.

If you have been sexually harassed at a co-op site, tell your co-op advisor and the Advocate. You can call to report the harassment from out-of-town at 1-800-841-1314.

If you have been victimized sexually in the past and you would like some assistance in working on these issues, there is help available. See a counselor at the Counseling Center or contact the Advocate or a peer advocate. If it's appropriate for you to see a therapist off-campus, we will try to help you find someone suitable. There are also support groups available each term for men and women who are survivors of sexual abuse.

There are ways to help prevent sexual violence on campus. A few tips:

- *Always* lock your room door when you're going to undress, sleep, or if you're under the influence of a substance which might impair your ability to react quickly. It's a good idea to get in the habit of locking your door whenever you're inside.

- *Never* prop outside doors open—strangers can enter buildings, as well as friends.

- If you're walking or running on the bike path at times when you might be the only one around, take a friend.

- Learn Self-Defense.

- Know your sexual desires and boundaries and communicate them clearly to any (potential) sexual partner; "listen" to your boundaries and honor them. If you're not sure, say "no" rather than "yes" or "maybe."

- Ask what a (potential) sexual partner's desires and boundaries are; listen to and respect them.

- If someone violates a sexual boundary, confront him/her on it. That may mean telling them directly, or, as a first step, talking with your hall advisor or HAC, the Advocate or a peer advocate, a counselor, or the Dean of Students.

The Antioch College Sexual Offense Policy
approved by the Board of Trustees in June 1992

All sexual contact and conduct on the Antioch College campus and/or occurring with an Antioch community member must be consensual.

When a sexual offense, as defined herein, is committed by a community member, such action will not be tolerated.

Antioch College provides and maintains educational programs for all community members, some aspects of which are required. The educational aspects of this policy are intended to prevent sexual offenses and ultimately to heighten community awareness.

In support of this policy and community safety, a support network exists that consists of the Sexual Offense Prevention and Survivors' Advocacy Program, an Advocate, Peer Advocates, and victim/survivor support groups through the Sexual Offense Prevention and Survivors' Advocacy Program and Counseling Services. The Advocate (or other designated administrator) shall be responsible for initiation and coordination of measures required by this policy.

The implementation of this policy also utilizes established Antioch governance structures and adheres to contractual obligations.

Consent

1. For the purpose of this policy, "consent" shall be defined as follows:

   the act of willingly and verbally agreeing to engage in
   specific sexual contact or conduct.

2. If sexual contact and/or conduct is not mutually and simultaneously initiated, then the person who initiates sexual contact/conduct is responsible for getting the verbal consent of the other individual(s) involved.

3. Obtaining consent is an on-going process in any sexual interaction. Verbal consent should be obtained with each new level of physical and/or sexual contact/conduct in any given interaction, regardless of who initiates it. Asking "Do you want to have sex with me?" is not enough. The request for consent must be specific to each act.

4. The person with whom sexual contact/conduct is initiated is responsible to express verbally and/or physically her/his willingness or lack of willingness when reasonably possible.

5. If someone has initially consented but then stops consenting during a sexual interaction, she/he should communicate withdrawal verbally and/or through physical resistance. The other individual(s) must stop immediately.

6. To knowingly take advantage of someone who is under the influence of alcohol, drugs and/or prescribed medication is not acceptable behavior in the Antioch community.

7. If someone verbally agrees to engage in specific contact or conduct, but it is not of her/his own free will due to any of the circumstances stated in (a) through (d) below, then the person initiating shall be considered in violation of this policy if:

   a) the person submitting is under the influence of alcohol or other substances supplied to her/him by the person initiating;

   b) the person submitting is incapacitated by alcohol, drugs, and/or prescribed medication;

   c) the person submitting is asleep or unconscious;

   d) the person initiating has forced, threatened, coerced, or intimidated the other individual(s) into engaging in sexual contact and/or sexual conduct.

Offenses Defined

The following sexual contact/conduct are prohibited under Antioch College's Sexual Offense Policy and, in addition to possible criminal prosecution, may result in sanctions up to and including expulsion or termination of employment.

RAPE: Non-consensual penetration, however slight, of the vagina or anus; non-consensual fellatio or cunnilingus.

SEXUAL ASSAULT: Non-consensual sexual conduct exclusive of vaginal and anal penetration, fellatio and cunnilingus. This includes, but is not limited to, attempted non-consensual penetration, fellatio, or cunnilingus; the respondent coercing or forcing the primary witness to engage in non-consensual sexual contact with the respondent or another.

SEXUAL IMPOSITION: Non-consensual sexual contact. "Sexual contact" includes the touching of thighs, genitals, buttocks, the pubic region, or the breast/chest area.

INSISTENT AND/OR PERSISTENT SEXUAL HARASSMENT: Any insistent and/or persistent emotional, verbal or mental intimidation or abuse found to be sexually threatening or offensive. This includes, but is not limited to, unwelcome and irrelevant comments, references, gestures or other forms of personal attention which are inappropriate and which may be perceived as persistent sexual overtones or denigration.

NON-DISCLOSURE OF A KNOWN POSITIVE HIV STATUS: Failure to inform one's sexual partner of one's known positive HIV status prior to engaging in high risk sexual conduct.

NON-DISCLOSURE OF A KNOWN SEXUALLY TRANSMITTED DISEASE: Failure to inform one's sexual partner of one's known infection with a sexually transmitted disease (other than HIV) prior to engaging in high risk sexual conduct.

Procedures

1. To maintain the safety of all community members, community members who are suspected of violating this policy should be made aware of the concern about their behavior. Sometimes people are not aware that their behavior is sexually offensive, threatening, or hurtful. Educating them about the effects of their behavior may cause them to change their behavior.

   If someone suspects that a violation of this Sexual Offense Policy may have occurred, she/he should contact a member of the Sexual Offense Prevention and Survivors' Advocacy Program or the Dean of Students.

   It is strongly encouraged that suspected violations be reported, and that they be reported as soon as is reasonable after a suspected violation has occurred. Where criminal misconduct is involved, reporting the misconduct to the local law enforcement agency is also strongly encouraged.

   Any discussion of a suspected violation with a member of the Sexual Offense Prevention and Survivors' Advocacy Program or the Dean of Students will be treated as confidential.

2. When a suspected violation of this policy is reported, the person who receives the report with the Sexual Offense Prevention and Survivors' Advocacy Program or the Dean of Students office will explain to the person reporting all of her/his options (such as mediation, the Hearing Board, and criminal prosecution) which are appropriate to the suspected offense.

3. If the person reporting a suspected policy violation wishes to arrange for mediation, then the Advocate, the Dean of Students, or a staff member of the Sexual Offense Prevention and Survivors' Advocacy Program shall arrange for mediation consistent with the mediation guidelines used by the Sexual Offense Prevention and Survivors' Advocacy Program.

   a) If the Dean of Students arranges mediation, the Dean shall notify the Advocate of the mediation session.

   b) A written agreement with educational and/or behavioral requirements may be part of the outcome of a mediation session. Copies of this agreement shall be given to the parties involved, the Advocate and the Dean of Students.

   c) Should a student persist in sexually threatening or offensive behavior after mediation has been attempted, the Sexual Harassment Committee or the Advocate should refer the case to the Hearing Board.

   d) If a satisfactory conclusion is not reached through mediation, or if the mediation agreement is not adhered to by any of its participants, then the case may be referred to the Hearing Board.

4. In the event that an action taken by the Dean of Students regarding a sexual offense is appealed, the appeal shall be made to the Hearing Board.

5. If the primary witness wishes the Hearing Board to make a finding regarding an alleged policy violation, the primary witness must file a written complaint with the Advocate. The Advocate shall inform the primary witness of her/his rights regarding procedure and appeal under this policy.

6. When a written complaint is filed, if the respondent is an employee, the Advocate shall inform the President or the President's designee of the reported violation of the Sexual Offense Policy. The matter will be promptly investigated by the appropriate administrator or other supervisor with the assistance of the Advocate. If whatever review process appropriate to the employee results in a determination that the policy has been violated, then the remedy should be commensurate with the

seriousness of the violation, and procedures specified in College and University policies should be followed.

7. When an official report is filed, if the respondent is a student, then the following procedures shall be followed:

   A. The Advocate shall notify the Dean of Students, or another senior College official, who shall have the respondent report to the Dean of Students' office within a reasonable period of time, not to exceed the next business day the College is open that the respondent is on campus. When the respondent reports, the respondent will then be informed by the Advocate and/or the Dean of Students of the report of the sexual offense, the policy violation which is being alleged, and her/his rights regarding procedure and appeal. The respondent will be given an opportunity to present her/his side of the story at that time. If the respondent does not report as directed, then implementation of this policy shall proceed.

   B. Based on the information available, the Advocate, or the Dean of Students in the Advocate's absence, will determine whether there is reasonable cause to believe that a policy violation may have occurred.

   C. In the event that the respondent is situated on campus, if (1) there is reasonable cause to believe that a policy violation may have occurred, and (2) there is reasonable cause to believe that the respondent may pose a threat or danger to the safety of the community, the Hearing Board will be convened as soon as possible, preferably within 24 hours from the time of the report to the Advocate, to determine whether the respondent shall be removed from campus until the conclusion of the Hearing process. If the Hearing Board cannot be convened within 24 hours but there is reasonable cause as stated in (1) and (2) above, the Dean of Students, or the Advocate in the Dean of Students' absence, can act to remove the respondent from campus.

   If the respondent is living on-campus and is temporarily banned from campus, the College will help arrange housing if the respondent is unable to locate any on her/his own.

If the respondent is taking classes on-campus and is temporarily banned from attending classes, the College will help provide alternative instruction.

The emergency removal of the respondent from campus shall not constitute a determination that the respondent has violated this policy.

D. The Hearing Board will then convene for a Hearing, to hear the case. Consistent with this policy, the Hearing Board will take into account the primary witness's story, the respondent's story, witnesses, the past history of the respondent, and other relevant evidence, and will determine whether or not a policy violation has occurred and which aspect of the policy has been violated.

E. The Hearing shall take place as soon thereafter as is reasonable, no longer than seven days from the date of filing or the notification of the respondent, whichever is later, unless the Advocate determines that reasonable cause exists for convening the meeting at a later, still reasonable time, in which event the Advocate shall so notify the Chair of the Hearing Board.

F. If the primary witness chooses, she/he may have a representative at all hearings of the Hearing Board and/or through any appeals process. The primary witness's advocate is to provide advocacy and emotional support for the primary witness. When appropriate, if the primary witness chooses, the Advocate or a Peer Advocate may act as the primary witness's representative at all hearings of the Hearing Board and/or through any appeals process. The primary witness may also choose to have someone outside the Sexual Offense Prevention and Survivors' Advocacy Program serve as her/his representative. Choosing a representative from within the Antioch community is encouraged.

G. If the respondent chooses, she/he may have a representative at all hearings of the Hearing Board and/or through any appeals process. The respondent's advocate is to provide advocacy and emotional support for the respondent. When appropriate, if the respondent chooses, the respondent may select an advocate from the list maintained by the Dean of Students' office of administrators and tenured faculty who have agreed to serve in this role. This advocate may act as the respondent's representative at all hearings of the Hearing Board and/or through any appeals process.

The respondent may also choose to have someone outside this list serve as her/his representative. Choosing a representative from within the Antioch community is encouraged.

8. The Hearing Board and any appellate body which hears a case under this policy shall administer its proceedings according to these fundamental assumptions:

A. There will be no reference to the past consensual, non-violent sexual contact and/or conduct of either the primary witness or the respondent.

B. No physical evidence of a sexual offense is necessary to determine that one has occurred, nor is a visit to the hospital or the administration of a rape kit required. The primary witness shall be supported by the Advocate in whatever decisions she/he makes, and be informed of legal procedures regarding physical evidence.

C. The fact that a respondent was under the influence of drugs or alcohol or mental dysfunction at the time of the sexual offense will not excuse or justify the commission of any sexual offense as defined herein, and shall not be used as a defense.

9. This policy is intended to deal with sexual offenses which occurred in the Antioch community, and/or with an Antioch community member, on or after February 8, 1991. Sexual offenses which occurred prior to that date were still a violation of community standards, and should be addressed through the policies and governance structures which were in effect at the time of the offense.

The Hearing Board

1. The Hearing Board's duties are:

a) to hear all sides of the story;

b) to investigate as appropriate;

c) to determine if a violation of this policy has occurred;

d) to develop, in consultation with the Dean of Students and the Advocate, an appropriate remedy in cases where mandatory remedies are not prescribed in this policy;

e) to prepare a written report setting forth its findings which it distributes to the parties involved and the Dean of Students.

2. The Hearing Board will consist of three community representatives as voting members and the Dean of Students as an ex-officio member.

3. By the end of each Spring quarter, nine representatives will be chosen to form a Hearing Board pool to begin serving at the beginning of the next academic year (Fall quarter) for the duration of that academic year: three each from the categories of students, faculty, and administrators/staff members.

A. The nine members of the Hearing Board pool shall be appointed by ADCIL from the following recommended candidates.

1) Six students recommended by COMCIL;

2) Six faculty members recommended by the Dean of Faculty and FEC;

3) Six administrators/staff members who shall be recommended by the President of the College.

B. At least five members of the Hearing Board pool shall be women.

C. Three of the representatives shall be appointed by ADCIL to serve each quarter as a Hearing Board. One Hearing Board member must be from each of the three categories listed above, and at least one member must be a person of color.

For every case which is heard, at least one Hearing Board member must be the same sex as the primary witness, and at least one Hearing Board member must be the same sex as the respondent.

D. One member of the Hearing Board shall be designated by ADCIL to serve as Chair. The Chair shall preside for all Hearing Board meetings that quarter, and shall make the necessary physical arrangements to convene the Hearing Board (i.e., contact Hearing Board members, notify all parties involved of date, time, place, etc.).

E. The six representatives who are not serving in a particular quarter shall be alternates in case an active member is not available or has a conflict of interest.

F. If an active member of the Hearing Board has a conflict of interest in the case, that member is responsible to report the conflict as soon as possible. ADCIL shall be responsible to determine if the conflict requires replacing the member, with an alternate chosen by ADCIL to immediately take her/his place. If convening ADCIL for this purpose would serve to delay the Hearing Board process, then the President shall make a determination regarding conflict and, if necessary, appoint an alternate.

4. All members of the Hearing Board pool shall receive training by the Advocate and the College attorney regarding this policy and pertinent legal issues.

5. The Hearing Board is expected to follow the procedures outlined in Appendix D. Any procedures not covered in this policy, including Appendix D, shall be determined according to the discretion of the Hearing Board.

Remedies

1. When a policy violation by a student is found by the Hearing Board, the Hearing Board shall also determine a remedy which is commensurate with the offense, except in those cases where mandatory remedies are prescribed in this policy.

   When a remedy is not prescribed, the Hearing Board shall determine the remedy in consultation with the Dean of Students and the Advocate, and shall include an educational and/or rehabilitation component as part of the remedy.

2. *For Rape:* In the event that the Hearing Board determines that the violation of rape has occurred, as defined under this policy, then the respondent must be expelled immediately.

3. *For Sexual Assault:* In the event that the Hearing Board determines that the violation of sexual assault has occurred, as defined under this policy, then the respondent must: a) be suspended immediately for a period of no less than six months; b) successfully complete a treatment program for sexual offenders approved by the Director of Counseling Services before returning to campus; and c) upon return to campus, be subject to mandatory class and co-op scheduling so that the respondent and primary witness avoid, to the greatest extent possible, all contact, unless the primary witness agrees otherwise.

   In the event that the Hearing Board determines that a second violation of sexual assault has occurred, with the same respondent, then the respondent must be expelled immediately.

4. *For Sexual Imposition:* In the event that the Hearing Board determines that the violation of sexual imposition has occurred, as defined under this policy, then the recommended remedy is that the respondent: a) be suspended immediately for a period of no less than three months; b) successfully complete a treatment program for sexual offenders approved by the Director of Counseling Services before returning to campus; and c) upon return to campus, be subject to mandatory class and co-op scheduling so that the respondent and primary witness avoid, to the greatest extent possible, all contact, unless the primary witness agrees otherwise.

   In the event that the Hearing Board determines that a second violation of sexual imposition has occurred, with the same respondent, then the recommended remedy is that the respondent: a) be suspended immediately for a period of no less than six months; b) successfully complete a treatment program for sexual offenders approved by the Director of

Counseling Services before returning to campus; and (c) upon return to campus, be subject to mandatory class and co-op scheduling so that the respondent and primary witness avoid, to the greatest extent possible, all contact, unless the primary witness agrees otherwise.

In the event that the Hearing Board determines that a third violation of sexual imposition has occurred, with the same respondent, then the respondent must be expelled immediately.

5. *For Insistent and/or Persistent Sexual Harassment:* In the event that the Hearing Board determines that the violation of insistent and/or persistent sexual harassment has occurred, as defined under this policy, then the recommended remedy is that the respondent: a) be suspended immediately for a period of no less than six months; b) successfully complete a treatment program for sexual offenders approved by the Director of Counseling Services before returning to campus; and c) upon return to campus, be subject to mandatory class and co-op scheduling so that the respondent and primary witness avoid, to the greatest extent possible, all contact, unless the primary witness agrees otherwise.

In the event that the Hearing Board determines that a second violation of insistent and/or persistent sexual harassment has occurred, with the same respondent, then the respondent must be expelled immediately.

6. *For Non-Disclosure of a Known Positive HIV Status:* In the event that the Hearing Board determines that there has been non-disclosure of a known positive HIV status, as defined under this policy, then the recommended remedy is that the respondent be expelled immediately.

7. *For Non-Disclosure of a Known Sexually Transmitted Disease:* In the event that the Hearing Board determines that there has been non-disclosure of a known sexually transmitted disease, as defined under this policy, then the recommended remedy is that the respondent be suspended immediately for a period of no less than three months.

In the event that the Hearing Board determines that there

has been a second failure to disclose one's known sexually transmitted disease, as defined under this policy, then the recommended remedy is that the respondent be suspended immediately for a period of no less than six months.

In the event that the Hearing Board determines that there has been a third failure to disclose one's known sexually transmitted disease, as defined under this policy, then the recommended remedy is that the respondent be expelled immediately.

8. In all cases, *a second offense* under this policy, regardless of category, must receive a more severe consequence than did the first offense if the second offense occurred after the Hearing Board's first finding of a respondent's violation of this policy.

9. The remedy for *a third offense* of this policy, regardless of category, must be expulsion, if the third offense occurred after the Hearing Board's first or second finding of a respondent's violation of this policy.

10. It is the responsibility of the Dean of Students to ensure that the Hearing Board's remedies are carried out.

The Appeals Process

1. In the event that the respondent or primary witness is not satisfied with the decision of the Hearing Board, then she/he shall have the right to appeal to the Hearing Board's decision within seventy-two hours of receiving that decision.

2. In the event of an appeal, the College shall secure the services of a hearing review officer with experience in conducting arbitrations or administrative agency or other informal hearings. A hearing review officer, who is not a current member of the Antioch College community, shall be selected by ADCIL in consultation with the Advocate for the purpose of handling such appeals.

3. The hearing review officer shall review the record(s) and/or written report(s) of the Hearing, any briefs or other written materials supplied to her/him by any of the involved parties, and

meet with any of the involved parties which she/he determines appropriate, to determine if there was fundamental fairness in the Hearing process.

The hearing review officer's analysis shall include a determination of whether the respondent was fully apprised of the charges against her/him; that the appealing party had a full and fair opportunity to tell her/his side of the story; and whether there was any malfeasance by the Hearing Board. The hearing review officer will present her/his findings and recommendation for action, if any, to the President of the College.

Confidentiality

1. All of the proceedings of the Hearing Board, and all testimony given, shall be kept confidential.

2. For the duration of the Hearing process and any appeals process, the primary witness, the respondent, and any witnesses coming forward shall have the right to determine when and if their names are publicly released. No one shall make a public release of a name not their own while the process is underway. Any public breach of confidentiality may constitute a violation of community standards and be presented to the Community Standards Board for debate.

    A. The name of the primary witness shall not be considered public knowledge until such time that the primary witness releases her/his name publicly.

    B. The name of the respondent shall not be considered public knowledge until such time that the respondent releases her/his name publicly, unless the respondent is found in violation of the policy, at which time the release of the respondent's name may be included with the release of the Hearing Board's findings. The name of the respondent will be released with the Hearing Board's findings if a violation is found and the remedy includes the suspension or expulsion of the respondent.

    C. The names of any witnesses who testify to the Hearing Board shall not be released publicly until such time that each witness chooses to release her/his own name publicly.

3. In the event of an appeal, the appealing party (or the party considering the appeal) shall have the right to review any written and/or audio records of the hearing. Such review shall take place on the Antioch campus with a member of the Hearing Board present. No materials are to be duplicated by any party; no materials are to be removed from the Antioch campus except to be given to the hearing review officer or to the College attorneys.

4. All members of the Hearing Board, including any note-takers, are bound to keep the contents of the proceedings confidential.

5. All written and/or audio records of the process which are kept by the Hearing Board are to be turned over to the College Attorneys at the conclusion of the appeals process, and shall be stored in their offices, to be disposed of when and as they see fit.

Educational and Support Implementation Procedures

1. A minimum of one educational workshop about sexual offenses, consent, and the nature of sexual offenses as they pertain to this policy will be incorporated into each quarterly orientation program for new students. This workshop shall be conducted by the Advocate or by a person designated by the Advocate. Attendance shall be required of all students new to the Antioch community.

2. Workshops on sexual offense issues will also be offered during all study quarters. The content of these workshops shall be determined by the Advocate. Each student shall be required to attend at least one workshop each academic year for which she/he is on campus for one or more study quarters, effective Fall 1992. Attendance records shall be maintained, and given to the Registrar's office. This requirement must be completed for graduation [pending approval by the faculty].

   a. It is recommended to the faculty that it develop a policy encouraging all faculty members to attend workshops on sexual offenses.

   b. Further, it is recommended to the College and University

administration that all employees working on the Antioch College campus be encouraged to attend workshops on sexual offenses.

3. A one-credit P.E. self-defense course with an emphasis on women's self-defense will be offered each quarter. This course should be open to all Antioch community members free of charge.

4. Permanent support groups for female and male survivors of sexual offenses will be established and maintained through Counseling Services and/or the Sexual Offense Prevention and Survivors' Advocacy Program.

5. A Peer Advocacy Program will be maintained that shall consist of both female and male community members, recruited and trained by the Advocate. The Peer Advocates shall provide information and emotional support for sexual offense victims/ survivors and primary witnesses. The peer advocates shall work with the Advocate in educating the community about sexual offenses and sexual wellness.

6. A support network for students who are on Co-op will be maintained by the Advocate and the Sexual Offense Prevention and Survivors' Advocacy Program, with trained crisis contact people available.

* * * * *

For your information:

The Sexual Offense Prevention and Survivors' Advocacy Program is located on the first floor of North Hall, through the center doors. Their telephone number is (513) 767-6459. On campus, call PBX 6459.

The 24-hour Sexual Offense Crisis and Support Line is PBX 6458 on campus; from off-campus, call (513) 767-6458 or 1-800-841-1314.

The Dean of Students' Office can also provide information about this policy. On campus, call PBX 6318. From off-campus, call (513) 767-6318.

Appendix 2

The Antioch Response:
Sex, You Just Don't Talk About It

Alan E. Guskin

Playing By Antioch's Rules (*New York Times* Op-Ed, December 26, 1993); No Huggy, No Kissy at This School (Associated Press, September 9, 1993); The Eyes May Say Yes, But the Lips Have to Give OK (*USA Today,* September 10–12, 1993); Antioch Sets New Standard of Sexual Equality (*Boston Globe,* Ellen Goodman, September 23, 1993)—all newspaper headlines challenging the reader about a two-year-old sexual consent policy at a small liberal arts college in Ohio. National attention for a college policy, even one about sex, is hard to believe. None of the stories were reporting on rape, sexual deviance, violence or any sordid behavior; they were re-

This piece was released as an Antioch College publication dated March 21, 1994. It was distributed to all Antioch alumni, students, and parents of students and was available to anyone requesting a copy. It is reprinted here courtesy of Alan E. Guskin, currently Chancellor of Antioch University. At the time it was written, Guskin was President of Antioch College.

porting on an educational policy dealing with sexual interaction between students, which states that students must seek verbal consent from a sexual partner at each level of sexual interaction.

National columnists wrote lengthy pieces, most making fun of the policy but a good number taking the sexual consent policy very seriously—Ellen Goodman devoted two thoughtful and positive columns exploring the new standard of sexual equality. The *New York Times,* the first major newspaper to visit the campus, devoted a thoughtful and well-written front-page article (September 25, 1993) to the policy after three full days of campus interviews with students and administrators, an editorial (October 11, 1993), a full column in the Sunday Magazine, an op-ed piece (Sunday, December 26, 1993), and two positive letters from readers. Saturday Night Live satirized the policy; *Time* magazine quoted verbatim from the policy, more to make fun of it but with some element of seriousness; the *Washington Post,* after printing an opinion piece by me, sent an inept reporter who sensationalized the issue beyond recognition.

Newsweek twice dealt with Antioch's policy, once as part of a piece challenging "sexual correctness," and in a separate piece on the College which portrayed the students as sexually active but very much committed to the mutual sexual consent policy. In the style of *Newsweek,* and most of the media, there is an emphasis on sensationalizing the sexual behavior of some students as if it were representative of all students.

Front-page stories appeared in the *London Times* and the *Bangkok Post,* as well as other newspapers in a number of countries, and crews arrived from Swiss Television, Australian 60 Minutes and the British Broadcasting Corporation. Stories appeared in almost every major newspaper in the United States and numerous local papers. There were scores of live interviews and discussions on radio and TV talk shows. TV reports appeared on every major network, including a segment on Eye to Eye with Connie Chung and a CNN report that ran continuously one weekend.

Daily, for over three months, television news cameras, reporters, producers, and photographers roamed the small campus searching for yet a new "angle" on this story. One national reporter, even more cynical than the rest, couldn't quite believe the two days of interviews with students and their near uniform acceptance of "their" policy.

I received irate letters—some unsigned, some from alumni, mostly from men—absurd, silly, outrageous: "I'm not going to give any more money." About one in five alums called as part of our fund-raising efforts reacted negatively—sometimes emotionally—to the policy. How can Antioch, the bastion of freedom, do such a thing? I also received many positive letters.

Wow! All this about a policy developed by students at a small college to deal with problems students are facing.

The public reaction is so out of keeping with the intentions of the students and others of us involved in the development of the policy that it cries out for discussion. Why are people so upset by sexual consent? Why are so many so ready to reject the Antioch policy without any discussion with the people at Antioch? Why the nasty letters about a policy that only deals with campus life and developing standards for brief and transitory sexual encounters of 18–25-year-olds in a college residential setting? Why the almost juvenile search for student modeling of the policy by so many TV reporters? Why the search for bizarre student behavior by many reporters only to sensationalize the behavior of a few students rather than accept the seriousness of the majority of Antioch students? And, more positive and interesting, why are the usually hardened national reporters willing to spend time off the record sharing their views with me about sexual issues?

How can it be that this simple, explicit policy, developed by students for student sexual interaction, has become the most widely reported university news story on higher education in memory? How can the story continue in the national media for over four months? What deep-seated feelings are touched, what issues joined?

Obviously, the reaction to the Antioch policy is all about sex! Surely, sex sells, but these are only words, no pictures, no steamy narrative, only cold policy-type words. I believe it's not just sex that has created the reaction, but the Antioch requirement that students talk about sex! Talking about it with someone whom you desire; getting consent before having sex; having to think about sexual acts that you are about to do; communicating with a partner about your interests—outrageous, silly, anti-romantic, puritanical, unworkable, it will reduce men's desire.

While there has been criticism and much fun poked at Antioch's policy, there have also been many who support the notion of sexual consent, at colleges and universities throughout the country and in the media. A letter to the editor in *The New Yorker* read:

> The November 29th Comment discusses Antioch College's rules requiring explicit verbal consent for each level of sexual intimacy. It is no punishment to put desire into words. Antioch's subtle and imaginative mandate is an erotic windfall: an opportunity for undergraduates to discover that wordplay and foreplay can be happily entwined; the chance to reinvent privately the joyless, overexposed arena called "sexual intimacy." What man or woman on Antioch's campus, or elsewhere, wouldn't welcome the direct question "May I kiss the hollow of your neck?" The possibilities are wonderful—pedagogic, even—as is the idea that language is choice.
>
> Julia A. Reidhead
New York City

Antioch is a very special small college known for its innovative programs, its progressive values, its free-spirited students and its willingness to take risks. But this story is only partly about the open-mindedness of Antioch and its students. The reaction to this policy on sexual consent is more about the difficulty people—including reporters and editors—have understanding what is really happening to young people on our college and university campuses, even those who have children in college and who were sexually active themselves when they were students in the 1960s.

The 1990s and the 1960s/1970s

While critics and satirists may make points and cute statements, the pain of date rape and unhappy sexual encounters continue to tear campuses apart. Date rape is not a simple matter easily discounted by women's refusal to take responsibility for their own behavior or to accept the reality of a bad night. Whether one assumes that 10 or 25 percent of college women have experienced date rape, the reality is that many college women are experiencing

serious abuse, that many college men are being abusive and sometimes accused and humiliated, and that the friends of each are suffering as well. Any campus policy that begins to deal with these
difficulties and does it in a healthy, helpful manner is worthy of
consideration.

National columnist Ellen Goodman reminds her readers in one
of her two columns on the Antioch policy:

> The point of the talk of sexual consent is, first of all, to pro-
> tect women from violence. But the freedom from violence,
> from the fear of forced sex, is itself a first step towards sex-
> ual pleasure. Mutual sexual pleasure.

Freedom? Yes, the Antioch sexual consent policy is about individual freedom, just as the Antioch policies and perspectives in
the 1950s, 1960s and 1970s were about individual freedom. Thirty
to forty years ago the issue was student freedom from parental
rules, where colleges and universities were setting themselves up
as a controlling parent, establishing rules regarding sexual relationships. This led to the sexual experimentation of the 1960s. Sex
on campus in the 1990s as compared to the 1960s is less mysteri-
ous to the sexually experienced high school graduates; after all,
over two-thirds of all entering first year students on campuses
throughout the country have had sex prior to their arrival at college. Casual sexual interaction on campuses throughout the country is commonplace. Sex today is also more deadly due to AIDS.

Today, the sexual freedom concerns of college students are not
about having sex, but who controls sexual relationships. The students of the 1990s were born in the 1970s amid the revolution for
women's rights and freedoms. Most girls who grew into college-
age women in the 1990s have a very different conception of sexual
encounters than their counterparts in the 1960s and 1970s and
most of the men of the 1990s. Freedom for the 1990s woman is the
freedom to determine how she uses her body. Women feel free to
initiate sex and expect their partner to respect their desire to stop
action whenever they choose. While the socialization of males has
not kept pace with that of females, both genders are grappling with
new roles in sexual behavior.

Sexuality as a Defining Issue

Sexual freedom of the 1990s is all about being able to have sexual relationships in the way that both people involved would like it to be. There is a great sense of security for each partner to know that their wishes will be honored and that they will not be accused of misinterpreting the other's sexual boundaries.

We must face directly what today's college students are telling us: that dealing with sexual matters in an open and direct manner is a defining issue for students of the 1990s. If there are doubts, a recent *USA Today* and MTV survey found that over 78 percent of the respondents who were between the ages of 16 and 29 thought that verbal consent regarding sexual behavior was desirable; the reason they gave was that such consent would help clear up miscommunication between partners. This finding held up for men (70 percent) and women (78 percent), African Americans (72 percent), Hispanics (82 percent) and whites (73 percent).

It is in this setting that sexual freedom and sexual consent are directly related to each other. To the man who thinks "Why not?" in regard to sexual intercourse, and to the woman who thinks "why?" sexual consent means communication that leads each down the same path. That path, I believe, is more romantic and more passionate for both partners.

To the people who desire to satisfy themselves whether or not they are sure their partner feels the same way, sexual consent is not a freedom but a restraint. As one man at Antioch said when he first heard about the sexual consent policy, "This policy means I can't get what I want when I want it." He is right! But is this freedom or license?

And, then there is safe sex and AIDS. The freedom to be safe requires talking about past sexual behavior and about whether or not one's partner has AIDS or a sexually transmitted disease. It is also about being able to protect oneself with condoms even if it isn't the most romantic, passionate or comfortable thing. Talking about sex and sexual consent requires having to ask uncomfortable questions, but in the 1990s this is a life-saving skill.

The generation of the 1990s is confronting us with their sexuality. What would have been promiscuous behavior even in the 1960s is pretty much normal sexual activity on campuses today—and anyone over 40 who opens their eyes will be enlightened.

Why Antioch?

It is not by chance that Antioch College created this policy and that the reaction of the media has focused on this small campus. Antioch students have been free spirits for many decades, and the campus governance system, which invests students with enormous responsibility in the decision-making process, enhances the likelihood that student issues will not only be talked about but acted upon. For years, Antioch students have been bringing to the campus cutting-edge issues for their generation—whether from their high school or from their work experiences around the country that they alternate with on campus studies every three months. Now in the 1990s this open sexual environment has created a new wave of freedom dealing with consensual sexual relationships.

The development of the Antioch policy in the Fall of 1990 was prompted by students' need to face the realities of the 1990s and the feelings they have about their right to choose how and when to use their bodies. The policy deals with the creation of community standards to avoid the pain of date rape and unhappy sexual encounters in an environment in which sexual activity is common and easily accepted. And it focuses on standards of healthy interaction, not the policing of people.

Most surprising to many people is that Antioch students initiated the development of this policy and were critical players in each step of its creation and revision. It is clear to me that if this were not a student-developed policy it would not have been accepted by the students. And it is widely accepted at Antioch College.

Personal Reflection and the Role of University Leaders

But while the students developed the policy, many adult, nonstudent members of the Antioch community actively participated in its development, especially the members of the College's executive council. As the Chair of that group, the Administrative Council (AdCil), it often fell to me to articulate the policy as it was being developed and to work with a number of critical students and faculty in bridging the huge differences of opinion. It fell to me, a "straight white man" in "power," to convince angry women students, a number of whom were not fond of men in general, especially those in powerful positions, that not only were we going to follow the democratic procedures of AdCil, but we were also going to follow the laws of the State of Ohio. The University's attorneys sat at the table and gave the students a short course on the fairness doctrine.

We all struggled to separate the real substantive issues from the anger and the attempted intimidation. All of the faculty and administrators on AdCil, who represented eight of the eleven members (students represent the other three), thought deeply about the pain being expressed by the students and the need to be fair to both the accused and the accuser. All of the nonstudents struggled with the explicitness of the language.

For me, especially, the sexual explicitness was difficult, not because of any prudishness—nobody has ever accused me of that—but because it fell to me as Chair of AdCil to voice publicly paragraph by paragraph the sexually explicit language. While there were no words in the policy that I had not heard or read, to read them in a serious way in public week after week taxed even my very high levels of tolerance for embarrassment.

I spent a good deal of time talking to my 21-year-old daughter, who was a student on campus. My daughter and I had agreed that we would not talk about campus matters, and we almost never violated that agreement. But on this issue we did talk. She was clearly heterosexual and had a good number of male friends. We discussed some of her sexual relationships openly and I learned a great deal about the life of students.

I learned that the policy was important, but I couldn't help seeing the pain it could cause. But then I also saw the pain that not having a policy could cause.

I thought long and hard about the issues of the fairness, about whether we were developing a good policy—which I believe happened—or being politically expedient in the context of very strong and strident student voices. I thought then and now about the charge of "male-bashing." Was all of this male-bashing women getting even, or was it that life was no longer as comfortable for male students as it had always been? One woman Antioch Trustee may have summed it up when she said that the men may be experiencing what she as a woman had always experienced in college: that life wasn't always easy, that she had to watch out for herself, and that she wasn't always comfortable. I agree with her. Antioch College is no longer a male-dominant environment where men feel free to do whatever they choose. But it is also not a female-dominant campus.

I also thought long and hard about the meaning of university leadership in the 1990s. The paradoxes for campus leaders in dealing with student sexual behavior are ever present:

- We can't legislate student sexual behavior, but we must forge a policy regarding student sexual behavior.
- We must provide the leadership to make sure that a policy is developed, but we must be sure that it is articulated by students.
- We must talk with student leaders and especially women with a strong interest in these issues, yet the most active, and probably most knowledgeable, students and faculty are most suspicious of the motives of leaders.
- We must develop a policy in an open process in which students and interested faculty are directly involved, yet dealing with these volatile issues—like date rape—could expose the institution to negative publicity regarding events that were previously hidden, unaddressed, or even unknown.
- We must collaborate on the development of a policy that will create positive community expectations about healthy sexual behavior, yet we will be inundated with deeply disturbing examples of the breakdown of healthy sexual relationships and the need to include protection against sexual abuse.

Leadership in this area is difficult and painful because of what we learn about the depths of experiences and pain of our students and because of the way we are treated. Even the most well-meaning leader will be treated with barely disguised hostility; the student advocates will assume that the president and other administrators represent the "tyranny of silence" that has surrounded sexual abuse on university campuses. Some of these students will become so intensely emotional that they say things they would later regret and probably forget, even though it will be difficult for me to erase it from my mind. As symbols or live people, university leaders have to struggle with being perceived as part of the problem until a viable solution is developed.

It is also extremely sensitive work because we are working on the edge of what we understand as older adults and in areas that have been off limits to institutional policies for over three decades. And while I may be a university leader, I am a human being who shares some of the taboos about sexual matters and about intervening in this area of student life.

The sexual-consent part of the policy, which emerged after six months of revisions to the original policy, brought a sense of relief to many of us—now we had a policy that truly focused on healthy human relationships and not on policing prohibited behavior; it focused on educating students about standards of behavior, not on acting like a government agency.

But I must admit that the process of developing this policy was grueling work. In its entirety, it took place in two phases over a fourteen-month period. It was personally the most painful process I've experienced in my nineteen years as a chancellor and president of two universities. And given my experiences, that says a lot.

Meaning for an Antioch Education

What does all this say about Antioch College and an Antioch education? First, the development and implementation of the policy is in Antioch's time-honored tradition of challenging accepted standards and staking out new directions on the frontier of an issue. Antioch is once again providing leadership to the rest of higher education. This policy of mutual sexual consent will become, in one form or another, part of behavioral standards in most colleges and universities. It is interesting to note that we did not seek out this publicity—it occurred two years after the policy was first developed.

Second, an Antioch education is built around our commitment to educating students to make a difference in the world by being agents of change for the creation of a humane and just society. The development of this policy and its implementation is about students trying to create a more humane, safe and healthy sexual environment on campus.

Third, an Antioch education is very much about living in and governing a community. The development and implementation of this policy was a major educational event, and remains so—

namely, students learning how to use available governance processes to take charge of their lives, and adult faculty and administrators working with them to realize their goals. The policy will continue to evolve with each new generation of students.

An Antioch education remains a powerful experience for those special few who have the strength and will to stay with it. I believe the graduates of Antioch in the 1990s will, because of their educational struggles, join the generations of very successful Antioch graduates who have indeed made a major contribution to this society by challenging accepted dogma and standards and by reaching for new conceptions and new victories for humanity.

Appendix 3

The Antioch Policy, a Community Experiment in Communicative Sexuality

Matthew R. Silliman

Antioch College, a small residential liberal arts college in Yellow Springs, Ohio, recently instituted a campus policy aimed at developing, in a social context, principles intriguingly similar to those Lois Pineau applies to legal remedies for date rape.[1] It is appropriate, even necessary, to survey that experiment here, for the success of any pro-active legal strategy, such as Pineau's, would depend on a concomitant development of social attitudes in practice. The law itself can certainly have an educative role, but given the amazing cacophony of ridicule, abuse, and aggressive ignorance which greeted news of the Antioch policy, Pineau's conclusion is probably too sanguine about the effectiveness of a mass media campaign for making such simple yet fundamental change. Educational institutions which address themselves to widespread social

1. Pineau, "Date Rape: A Feminist Analysis," reprinted as Chapter 1 of this book.

problems by developing community-based responses perform a critical function in trying out solutions, independently of whether those strategies could apply unmodified to the society as a whole.

This essay aims briefly to defend the reasonableness of the Antioch policy against several of the charges which have been leveled against it. My principal thesis is that anyone who subscribes to a minimalist version of the Enlightenment Liberal conceptions of freedom, consent, choice, and individual liberty ought to welcome both the process and the product of Antioch's efforts to confront the problem of sexual exploitation and acquaintance rape. It is an understatement to say that the policy has not, however, been received with welcome, leading to the suspicion either that its detractors do *not* subscribe to such principles or that it has been systematically misunderstood.

Among many criticisms, the policy has been called paternalistic and authoritarian, puritanical and neo-Victorian, an attempt to reduce sexual intimacy to contractual relations, artificial or anti-romantic, and unenforceable. These are not simple criticisms, but vigorous denunciations, and many of them come from alleged representatives of so-called mainstream culture. It is instructive to note the ferocity with which they are issued, for it may be an indication that the policy touches a nerve worthy of further probing. I will address each of these charges in turn; the more delicate task of examining deeper philosophical objections, specifically those concerns stemming from the problematicity of the above Liberal concepts, I will forgo in the present essay, except to indicate some of them in passing.

Paternalism

Detractors of the Antioch policy, which provides for a system of adjudication and sanctions for offenses ranging from nondisclosure of a known sexually transmitted disease to rape, have termed it paternalistic, even authoritarian, in scope and content. Those making such charges are apparently under the impression that the policy was imposed on the campus community by an administration excessively concerned with the personal morality of its students, and a particular concern to "protect" women from unwelcome sexual contact.

It is worth observing that to the extent that the policy is correctly described as paternalistic, it is certainly not more so than is the society at large with respect to those serious offenses (we do not usually speak of laws against battery, rape, murder, etc., as paternalistic). Antioch has at most slightly redefined the criteria for determining whether such an offense has been committed. However, the charge of paternalism misses a very important feature of Antioch's procedure in adopting the policy, a feature which suggests that it is actually much less paternalistic than is the wider society. The policy is the product of a long and inclusive process of community deliberation, initiated by students and giving all members of the college community a full and thorough deliberative role. Debate and discussion on committees, task forces, and open forums over a significant period of time were designed to ensure that the policy was not imposed autocratically and that its function in the community was more educative than punitive (in fact, few alleged violations have reached the point of implementing punishment).

Moreover, the policy makes a rare and important point of insisting, from the point of the original complaint, that the adjudicative process ". . . honor[s] the wishes of the victim regarding what is done (or not done)." This provision is expressly not a threat to the rights of the accused (who is also given specific protections), but is an attempt to ensure both that the victim is not revictimized by an impersonal process, and that the inherently autocratic process of enforcement avoids, to the extent possible, aggravating an already difficult situation.

The charge of paternalism or authoritarianism is, therefore, either rooted in ignorance of the policy itself, or based on a misunderstanding of the community process which gave rise to it. To make such a charge would thus be to confuse thoughtful decisions of an interactive community with anonymous dictates of an impersonal state. This is not to suggest that large-scale governments are incapable of thoughtful policy, or that Antioch is a utopian community without problematic power relations. Paternalism is probably alive and well at Antioch; in this policy it seems to be at low ebb.

Puritanism

Related to the charge of paternalism is the claim that the policy is puritanical or neo-Victorian, a return to the putative bad old days of colleges and universities serving *in loco parentis* to regulate the sexual behavior of their students. Several obvious features of the Antioch policy contradict this rather odd criticism. In the first place, the policy does not forbid any legal sexual practice; it does not attempt to tell students when, whether, or with whom to have or not to have sex. Although the policy was developed in response to serious concerns about the prevalence of women being raped by men, it acknowledges that sexual misconduct is possible in any intimate context, and is written so as to apply generically to women and men, lesbians, straights, bisexuals, and gays.

The policy simply and eloquently insists that consent—which is, after all, already required by existing state and federal law (and widely assented to as an appropriate principle in such matters)—be overt.[2] The college's motivation for this requirement is neither the prudish regulation of students' sexual lives nor a misguided attempt to regulate behavior "for their own good"; it stems instead from the collectively perceived threats to members of the community of rape and sexually transmitted disease. It is thus an essentially respectful attempt to address, in particular ways, the enormous and highly intractable social problem, which is also a *criminal* problem, of acquaintance rape, by the reasonable expedient of insisting that consent be verbally expressed and be an ongoing verbal process.

Contractualization of Intimacy

The Antioch policy does not, as many charge, make sexual relations contractual in the legal sense, thus illegitimately importing

---

2. Among the most problematic of Liberal concepts, of course, are those of consent and informed consent. I will not here defend them against the radical criticism that gendered socialization so circumscribes the lives, of women especially, that to speak of their free consent, particularly to heterosexual acts, is meaningless. This is a topic for a different essay. For the present I will say only (a) that consent is a powerful idea with which it is politic to work even as we critique it, and (b) that a charge of false consciousness logically implies that we can in principle distinguish it from some truer consciousness—that is, that it must be *possible* to overcome one's social programming (at least incrementally) and become freer, if never entirely free, of overwhelming socializing forces. Thus, while it makes eminent sense to question the "freedom" of a woman's "choice" to engage in heterosexual sex under patriarchy, we must also admit that such constraint admits of varying degrees and that the concept of consent is therefore merely complicated, not vacuous.

contract relations into putatively private, intimate spaces. Rather, what the requirement to solicit and verbalize consent or nonconsent at various stages of intimacy does is short-circuit a process whereby, in the prevailing mythology of sexual relations, a woman is presumed to have made a quasi-contractual (usually nonverbal) commitment to have sex by agreeing to one stage of physical intimacy, or by not actively resisting (thereby doing what she may believe will place her at further risk). As Pineau argues, socially (and even legally) a woman is often presumed to have generated a sort of contractual obligation to follow through sexually, even when her attire or behavior is merely interpreted (by someone else) as seductive. Under the Antioch principles, whether a rape victim did or did not "ask for it" becomes purely a matter of whether the defendant can plausibly claim that words to that effect were actually spoken, and not at all a matter of what mythological delusions were operative in the perpetrator's imagination. Such a claim, or its counterclaim, is significantly easier to test for plausibility in case a complaint requires adjudication.

The prevailing presumption of contractual obligation, which Antioch calls into question with its policy, is indefensible, both on the grounds that the law does not equate even a promise with a binding contract, and because it is rooted in a common but false empirical belief that male sexuality is not subject to rational or moral control. By insisting not only on verbal consent, but on a series of verbal consents at different stages of intimacy, the Antioch policy implicitly denies both the false belief about male sexuality and the invidious presumption of an obligation arising from a woman's prior words or actions. It is, as Pineau argues, the criterion of consent as it is presently interpreted which sets up a sexual encounter as contractually obligatory; the Antioch policy does the opposite.

Artificiality

The specific requirement that consensual sexual acts involve both a verbalization of consent and a process of renewed verbalization at subsequent levels of intimacy have led several observers to object that it seems to take all the spontaneity out of intimacy, that it seems somehow "artificial." It seems more than strange that any thoughtful person living in the present decade can still imagine sexual relations as having an obviously "natural," and thereby normative, pattern. This is strange not only because of what we have learned about cultural and historical differences in the construction of sexual meaning and practice, but also because what might have seemed natural a few years ago is now potentially lethal. Real changes in society and biology must lead to changes in how we live and love, and these changes will seem "artificial" only to those who do not acknowledge that the world is different from when they were younger.

That otherwise thoughtful people have expressed this as a criticism is, however, powerful testimony to the durability of patriarchal mythmaking about "human nature." As is usual when such claims are made, the rhetoric of nature here serves to enshrine the sexual status quo—a sexual double standard which undermines attempts to pose substantive solutions to serious social problems, such as the prevalence of acquaintance rape (shocking even by conservative estimates). Such an argument reveals itself to assume that these very real problems, especially those facing women, are simply not very important.

Associated with the charge of artificiality is the sense that being required to talk about intimacy while pursuing it is antiromantic and destructive of spontaneity. Several things might be said about this, ranging from the concern that romance and spontaneity may in some cases be inconsistent with adequate safety and respect for one's sexual partner(s), to the assertion that, in practice, once new habits are developed, sex in accordance with the Antioch policy need be no less spontaneous or emotionally affecting than otherwise, and perhaps more so, since possible ambiguities of communication between partners, relating to whether one or the other does or does not actually wish to be doing what they are doing, become significantly less likely.

It is difficult to imagine, however, what motivates the concern about spontaneity if not a fear of being held accountable for whether one's partner actually consents to a sexual act or not (one student at a state university was reported to protest, revealingly, that if he had to get verbal consent he would "never get to have sex"). Active and ongoing communication about sex certainly cannot eliminate the ambiguities, risks, doubts, and anxieties of sexuality in our society. It does, however, neutralize some of the guesswork, and it effectively undercuts much cultural mythology that is operative in sexual relations. This gives some reason to believe that such a practice could in fact lead to a *more* romantic and (in other ways) spontaneous experience.[3]

Unenforceability

Some have criticized the policy for being difficult or impossible to enforce, given that sexual acts normally occur in private. This is in one sense another species of the objection raised above about autocratic attempts to control personal morality, the replies to which I will not repeat. It also suggests a naiveté about the function in our lives of laws and rules generally.

Enforcement of any regulation is always a sort of rear-guard action, serving at best to remind potential violators of the risks of noncooperation as an adjunct to the many other motivations for obedience (habit, respect for authority, sense of community, perceived self-interest, etc.). Regulations work best when they merely codify an already nearly universal practice, or when their principal function is more educative than punitive, which the Antioch policy (as noted above) emphatically is. The policy itself provides for formal introduction to its terms and purposes for every new member of the community, and all indications so far are that the initiative has been overwhelmingly well-received by the student body.

Moreover, when we reflect that existing rape, sexual assault, and sexual harassment laws (which Antioch's policy supplements) are among the most difficult laws to enforce, precisely because the court must decide whether to believe the plaintiff or the defendant in the absence of much supporting evidence, the objection is once again turned on its head. By specifying overt, clear, verbal commu-

---

3. It is legitimate to object that this begs important questions about what constitutes or ought to constitute spontaneous, romantic, or desirable sex. Some would argue that whatever sex a person desires (or alternatively, *authentically* desires) is ipso facto desirable, and that it would be prima facie wrong to specify, even negatively, what forms this should take. This, again, is an issue I must decline to address in the present essay, except to say that if the person making such an objection has agreed with me that we have an identifiable problem of *bad* sex, that is, sex which is exploitative in one of a number of specifiable ways, then that person has already conceded at least a negative prescriptive criterion for sexuality. On the other hand, to deny that exploitative sex is a problem would entail denying even the conceptual possibility of rape.

nication as the criterion by which the presence or absence of consent is to be measured, the policy dramatically clarifies for people, in advance, what needs to have occurred for the defendant honestly to presume consent. With this clarification, it ought to be much more difficult for either party to lie plausibly about the specific dialogue accompanying the disputed encounter, and considerably easier to determine whether the event was a sexual offense or an honest misunderstanding. To the extent that enforceability is not merely a red herring, therefore, the Antioch policy should actually improve just enforcement.

Conclusion

It would be foolish to pretend that verbalizing consent eliminates the possibility (even, under patriarchy, the probability) of various forms of pressure and coercion, from threats and emotional manipulation to social conditioning and the emotional depredations of prior abuse (the Antioch policy makes specific reference to such abuse and provides for counseling and other resources to address it). This granted, however, who would argue that verbal consent, solicited and obtained, can have *no effect whatever* in relieving deep communicative ambiguity and undercutting damaging sexual mythology? That clear, direct language is an antidote to superstition and confusion is a basic tenet of the Liberal heritage, and although its efficacy can certainly be exaggerated, it would be difficult to argue that it has no place at all.

The Antioch policy seems to me also to go one step beyond this Liberal doctrine, in attempting to reformulate the meaning and power dynamic of consent in social practice, but it does so without undermining any commonly held liberal principle other than the indefensible myths of explicit patriarchy. It is not by any stretch of the imagination a conclusive solution to the social and criminal problems involved in sexual relations, but it does begin to address some real issues, in ways that building more prisons, prescribing harsh sentences for convicted rapists, and seeking to further restrict women's freedom of movement, the most common of proposed antidotes to rape, do not.

Antioch has long been recognized for its respectfulness of students making their own choices in social as well as academic areas, so it is not surprising, or a change of direction, as some al-lege, that this experiment arose at such an institution (an Antioch alumna of my acquaintance has gleefully nicknamed the college "U. Ask!"). Far from being a reversal of a respectful tradition or a threat to liberty, the new policy seems to be real, if incremental, progress toward the same ideal. If Antioch's policy impinges upon anyone's "liberty," it does so only in that it undermines the presumptive privilege of men to have their needs met without concern for the needs and feelings of women. This seems a small loss compared to the enormous probable gain in substantive freedom—from harassment and misunderstanding—for all members of the community.

I am grateful to Leslie Francis, Greta Phinney, David K. Johnson, and Lisa Tessman for their advice and encouragement on this project.

Selected Bibliography

Bachman, Ronet, and Raymond Paternoster. "A Contemporary Look at the Effects of Rape Law Reform: How Far Have We Really Come?" *Journal of Criminal Law and Criminology* 81 (1993), 554–74.

Balos, Beverly, and Mary Louise Fellows. "Guilty of the Crime of Trust: Nonstranger Rape," *Minnesota Law Review* 75 (1991), 599–619.

Beinen, Leigh. "National Developments in Rape Reform Legislation," *Women's Rights Law Reporter* 6 (1980), 170–213.

Berliner, Dana. "Rethinking the Reasonable Belief Defense to Rape," *Yale Law Journal* 100 (1991), 2687–706.

Bogart, J. H. "On the Nature of Rape," *Public Affairs Quarterly* 5 (1991), 117–36.

Bourque, Linda Brookover. *Defining Rape.* Durham, N.C.: Duke University Press, 1989.

Bownes, Ian T., Ethna C. O'Gorman, and Angela Sayers. "Rape—A Comparison of Stranger and Acquaintance Assaults," *Medicine, Science, and the Law* 31 (1991), 102–9.

Brownmiller, Susan. *Against Our Will: Men, Women, and Rape.* New York: Simon & Schuster, 1975.

Clark, Lorenne, and Debra Lewis. *Rape: The Price of Coercive Sexuality.* Toronto: Women's Press, 1977.

Coombs, Mary. "Telling the Victim's Story," *Texas J. Women and the Law* 2 (1993), 277–315.

Curley, E. M. "Excusing Rape," *Philosophy and Public Affairs* 5 (1976), 325–60.

Daly, Kathleen. "Criminal Justice Ideologies and Practices in Different Voices: Some Feminist Questions About Justice," *International J. Soc. L.* 17 (1989), 1.

Davis, Michael. "Setting Penalties: What Does Rape Deserve?" *Law and Philosophy* 3 (1984), 61–110.

Donovan, Dolores A., and Stephanie M. Wildman. "Is the Reasonable Man Obsolete? A Critical Perspective on Self-Defense and Provocation," *Loyola of Los Angeles Law Review* 14 (1981), 435–68.

Estrich, Susan. "Palm Beach Stories," *Law and Philosophy* 11 (1992), 5–33.

———. *Real Rape.* Cambridge: Harvard University Press, 1987.

Fairstein, Linda A. *Sexual Violence: Our War Against Rape.* New York: William Morrow, 1993.

Friedland, Steven I. "Date Rape and the Culture of Acceptance," *Florida Law Review* 43 (1991), 497–527.

Galvin, Jim. "Rape: A Decade of Reform," *Crime and Delinquency* 31 (1985), 163–68.

Gilbert, Neil. "Realities and Mythologies of Rape," *Society* 29 (1992), 4–10.

Griffin, Susan. *Rape: The Politics of Consciousness.* New York: Harper & Row, 1986.

Husak, Douglas N., and George C. Thomas III. "Date Rape, Social Convention, and Reasonable Mistakes," *Law and Philosophy* 11 (1992), 95–126.

Ingram, John Dwight. "Date Rape: It's Time for 'No' to Really Mean 'No,' " *American Journal of Criminal Law* 21 (1993), 3–36.

Koss, Mary. "Date Rape: The Story of an Epidemic and Those Who Deny It," *Ms. Magazine,* October 1985.

Kramer, Karen M. "Rule by Myth: The Social and Legal Dynamics Governing Alcohol-Related Acquaintance Rapes," *Stanford Law Review* 47 (1994), 115–60.

Levine, Sylvia, and Joseph Koenig, eds. *Why Men Rape.* Toronto: Macmillan, 1980.

MacKinnon, Catharine. *Feminism Unmodified: Discourses on Life and Law.* Cambridge: Harvard University Press, 1987.

———. *Toward a Feminist Theory of the State.* Cambridge: Harvard University Press, 1989.

Marsh, Jeanne C., Allison Geist, and Nathan Caplan. *Rape and the Limits of Law Reform.* Boston: Auburn House, 1982.

May, Larry, and Robert Strikwerda. "Men in Groups: Collective Responsibility for Rape," *Hypatia* 9 (1994), 134–51.

McGregor, Joan L. "Force, Consent, and the Reasonable Woman," in Jules

Coleman, ed., *In Harm's Way*. New York: Cambridge University Press, 1994.

"Men, Women and Rape," special issue on women and the law, *Fordham Law Review* 63 (1991), 125–73.

Olsen, Frances. "Statutory Rape: A Feminist Critique of Rights Analysis," *Texas Law Review* 53 (1984), 387–432.

O'Neill, Onora. "Between Consenting Adults," *Philosophy and Public Affairs* 14 (1985), 252–77.

Patel, Krishna R. "Recognizing the Rape of Bosnian Women as Gender-Based Persecution," *Brooklyn Law Review* 50 (1991), 929–58.

Pitch, Tamar. "Critical Criminology, the Construction of Social Problems, and the Question of Rape," *International Journal of the Sociology of the Law* 13 (1989), 35–46.

Posner, Richard. *Sex and Reason*. Cambridge: Harvard University Press, 1992.

Roiphe, Katie. *The Morning After: Sex, Fear, and Feminism on Campus*. New York: Little, Brown, 1993.

Scheppele, Kim. "The Re-vision of Rape Law," 54 *U. Chi. L. Rev.* 1095 (1987).

Schulhofer, Stephen J. "Taking Sexual Autonomy Seriously: Rape Law and Beyond," *Law and Philosophy* 11 (1992), 35–91.

Ward, Sally, et al. *Acquaintance and Date Rape: An Annotated Bibliography*. Westport, Conn.: Greenwood Press, 1994.

Warshaw, Robin. *I Never Called It Rape: The Ms. Report on Recognizing, Fighting, and Surviving Date and Acquaintance Rape*. New York: Harper & Row, 1988.

West, Allison. "Tougher Prosecution When the Rapist Is Not a Stranger: Suggested Reform to the California Penal Code," *Golden Gate University Law Review* 24 (1994), 169–88.

Contributors

DAVID M. ADAMS teaches philosophy at the California State Polytechnic University in Pomona. He is the author of *Philosophical Problems in the Law, 2nd ed.* (1996) and writes and has published in the areas of philosophy of law and legal theory, social philosophy, bioethics, and business ethics.

LESLIE PICKERING FRANCIS is professor of law and philosophy at the University of Utah. She received her Ph.D. from the University of Michigan and her J.D. from the University of Utah. She has published articles on issues of justice in health care and on affirmative action and is currently completing a book on sexual harassment as an ethical issue in academic life.

ALAN E. GUSKIN is currently Chancellor of Antioch University. At the time he wrote "The Antioch Response," he was President of Antioch College.

ANGELA P. HARRIS teaches criminal law and constitutional law at the University of California—Berkeley School of Law (Boalt Hall). Her research interests are in feminist and critical race theory, and she is currently at work on a book tentatively entitled "What We Talk About When We Talk About Race."

LOIS PINEAU has taught philosophy in both Canada and the United States. She has published articles in philosophy of language, political philosophy, feminist theory, and philosophy of law. In 1992 she left academia to take up a political position with the New Democratic government of Ontario. She has subsequently turned to the study of law and is presently reading for a law degree at the University of Toronto.

MATTHEW R. SILLIMAN is Associate Professor and Chair of the Philosophy Department at North Adams State College in Massachusetts. He holds a doctorate from Purdue University, has published on Locke, Hobbes, philosophy of law, and educational theory, and is presently at work on a book entitled "Civil Disobedience as Political Narrative."

CATHARINE PIERCE WELLS is currently Associate Dean of Academic Affairs and Professor of Law at The Boston College Law School. Formerly she was Professor of Law at the University of Southern California and an Assistant Attorney General for the Commonwealth of Massachusetts. She received her Ph.D. from the University of California at Berkeley and her J.D. from Harvard Law School. She teaches and writes in the fields of tort law, criminal law, and legal theory.

Index